RUNNING AGAINST THE WIND

Spiritual Support for this Challenging Race of Life

LEO CALVIN PRICE

CONTENTS

Opening Remarks		*5*
Prologue		*7*
Chapter One	RUNNING	*13*
Chapter Two	RUNNING IN THE DARKNESS	*20*
Chapter Three	YOU CAN'T OUT RUN YOU	*27*
Chapter Four	RUNNING WITH THE HORSES	*34*
Chapter Five	YOU CAN'T OUT RUN THE BULL	*42*
Chapter Six	RUNNING A FEVER	*51*
Chapter Seven	RUNNING INJURED	*62*
Chapter Eight	RUN WITH THE WIND	*73*
Chapter Nine	YOU DID RUN WELL	*81*
Chapter Ten	THE TRUTH ABOUT RUNNING	*91*
Chapter Eleven	NO EXCUSES	*98*
Chapter Twelve	RUNNING WITH GRACE	*107*
Chapter Thirteen	RUN DOWN	*117*
Epilogue		*128*
Source Page		*132*

OPENING REMARKS

I was probably around 12 years old running across a field with my dog Rex. It was on that kind of Missouri day that had all the *Tom Sawyer* kind of feelings: a soft warm breeze and white fluffy clouds that seemed to drift aimlessly across the sky. The kind of day that made you feel like you could run forever. It was impossible not to run. The day seemed to demand it. Everything seemed to demand it. The warmth and the wind demanded, *run*. While other events might make you want to hide, all of this made me want to run.

I could see Rex running, zigzagging, first one side and then the other, looking for only what he alone knew. His tail wagging and what appeared to be a smile on his face. In my mind now looking back he wasn't looking for anything, he was just having fun. I miss Rex.

We didn't have much in the way of things and gadgets, just this open field. But, man, we had a good time.

It seems like now it takes more to have a good time. Oh, I know, we're adults, with responsibilities, now. We have places we need to go and things we need to do and to top it all, I'm still running, at least in my mind. My mind races here and there doing this and thinking about that. Oh, yeah, I'm still running. I'm just not enjoying it. There's no warm breeze, no soft white fluffy clouds. This is not a Tom Sawyer kind of life now. Rex, where are you?

I'm starting to wonder why I run now.

I was running, flying, but now I'm tumbling head over heels. And this is gonna hurt. It makes no sense: the ground looked level, the grass looked level even the weeds looked level. I didn't see it. I didn't know it was there. The dip in the ground, the sudden change in topography. Oh it had been there all along; I just didn't know it. It was a bone-jarring experience. I can feel it even now. It knocked the breath out of me. Not so much fun now. Rex is licking my face as if to say, "Get up, quit goofing around. Let's go!" I don't feel so much like running now. I wonder if I ever will again. I was a kid then, I was resilient then. I just don't know about now... *What about you?*

I think I'll get up and try again. Can I? Will I? What about you?

Come on now, let's do it together. The words of Henry Ford come to mind, "If you think you can or if you think you can't... you're right." Remember *"The Little Engine that Could"*, that 1930 children's book by Platt & Munk? *"I think I can... I think I can."*

You know *I think* we can.

PROLOGUE

Since the life of Christ is every way most bitter to nature ... and the Self ... and the Me ... (for in the true life of Christ, the Self and the Me and nature must be forsaken and lost and die altogether), therefore in each of us, nature hath a horror of it.
Theologia Germanica, XX by Martin Luther 1516

There I am looking up that long narrow incline that appears as least in my mind to be miles long. The words of Martin Luther come to me; *"nature hath a horror of it."* I'm in a race but it's not against anyone I'm running against myself. This is perhaps the most difficult of all.

GOD'S creation of Adam's race has been appropriately named, race. Though in the context of this book it's not about ethnic background, education or how much you have in the bank. In this race of life there will be drama and darkness to deal with. In Christianity, Christ will be what you are ultimately running to or running from. You will either be running against what seems to have become in our era just a story with some kind of moralistic attribute or what seems to be nonsensical and conjured up by religious ideology. Telling a story, spinning a yarn, that's what the naysayers have proclaimed and the world believes this to be a fairy tale, an illusion for the disillusioned. Even more frightening is that many self-proclaimed Christians parrot this. For many Christians, to be a Christian means simply a good philosophy. It's a positive attitude. It's mental assent. This is one aspect you will be running against.

For others of us it will be running from that still small voice, that wind in willows as it were whispering; *"Come unto me and I will give you rest..."* Running from Christ will be difficult. Running to Christ you will find; *"My Peace I give to you."*

Who will you listen to? Remember, as I will often say; *"voices influence our choices."*

Sometime ago I read Robin R. Meyers book *"Saving Jesus From The Church"* he Pastors the Mayflower Congregational and is described as *"unapologetically Christian, unapologetically liberal,"* which gives impetus to this philosophy. *"I have never believed,"* Robin says, *"in the virgin birth as a biological fact, the infallibility of scripture as a test of faith, the miracles as past suspension of natural law demanding current suspension of reason, the blood atonement (that the suffering on the innocent can vicariously atone for the sins of the guilty) as the foreordained mission of Jesus, the bodily resurrection as the only way to understand Easter, or the second coming as necessary sequel – and I am the pastor of a church that does not define Christianity this way either"* (6) he adds, *"we are doing our best to avoid the worship of Christ and trying to get back to something much more fulfilling and transformative"* (6).

Robin quotes John Dominic Crossan at length: *"it is not enough, therefore, to keep saying that Jesus was not born of a virgin, not born of David's linage, not born in Bethlehem, that there was no stable, no shepherds, no star, no Magi, no massacre of the infants, and no flight into Egypt" (32).*

Robin characterizes Jesus as *"A Galilean sage evolved over time into a divine Savior" (35).* He continues, *"According to history's best guess, Jesus of Nazareth was born just before 4 BCE to Joseph and Mary in a tiny hamlet. He was perhaps the firstborn, but more likely not, and had at least six siblings. The rest is etiology and myth, adapted to convey important interpretive responses by Matthew and Luke to his remarkable life, written fifty to sixty years after his death. A beautiful, but obviously contrived, tale is the virgin birth, which may have been to cover a scandal" (40).*

There is in our world today an aggregate effort to diminish in any way possible the Christ of Calvary and to do that one must dismiss with disdain the narrative of the Bible as fabrication. It is with condescension that the creation story is dismissed, with a look of "you poor diluted, uninformed and illiterate, crutch seeking Christian." All this is meant to demean and discourage any plausible thought that the Adam story has any validity. Once these are discarded then the narrative of Christ and Calvary becomes easier to throw away and Nietzsche's *"God is dead"* philosophy takes hold.

The difficulty of doing away with the atonement through Christ at Calvary is that redemption *("redeem" means to rescue from sin and the penalties for violation of divine law)* understandably won't allow us to truly see ourselves. Redemption at the core of who we are reveals our wretchedness and that's an ugly picture.

Blaise Pascal, the renowned 17th century philosopher and mathematician whose approach to Christianity is thoroughly Christocentric, made an important observation. The Christian religion, he claimed, teaches these truths:
"That there is a God whom men are capable of knowing and that there is an element of corruption in men that renders them unworthy of God. Knowledge of God without knowledge of man's wretchedness begets... pride and... knowledge of man's wretchedness without knowledge of God begets... despair, but knowledge of Jesus Christ furnishes man's knowledge of both simultaneously."

More than 60 years ago, theologian H. Richard Niebuhr summarized the creed of an easygoing American Christianity, *"A God without wrath brought men without sin into a kingdom without judgment though the ministrations of a Christ without a cross."*

I still like the quote signed simply, Graffiti, that said:

"God is dead."
Nietzsche

The next line reads:
"Nietzsche is dead."
God

Excuse me; if it's all the same to you I think I'll just ***run this race*** with this Christ crowd, the resurrected Christ that is.

Stay In the Arena

It is not the critic who counts, not the man who points out how the strong man stumbled or where the doer of deeds could have done better.

The credit belongs to the man who is actually in the arena; whose face is marred by dust and sweat and blood; who strives valiantly; who errs and comes short again and again; who knows the great enthusiasms, the great devotions, and spends himself in a worthy cause; who, at the best, knows in the end the triumph of high achievement; and who, at the worst, if he fails, at least fails while daring greatly, so that his place shall never be with those cold and timid souls who know neither victory nor defeat.

Excerpt from the speech by Theodore Roosevelt "Citizenship In A Republic" delivered at the Sorbonne, in Paris, France on 23 April, 1910

Chapter One

RUNNING

The air was cold and crisp, so I pulled down my red stocking cap around my ears. Zipped up my Nike thermal running pullover and slipped on my gloves. This was going to be a good run. The sun was shining; the sky was clear and blue. It felt invigorating. The atmosphere was filled with energy. This was going to be enjoyable. I had already mapped out my route, but I have now, however, decided to take a longer route because such a glorious day mandates nothing less.

Ah! What was it the Scottish poet Robert Burns said?

"The best-laid plans o' mice an' men
Gang aft a-gley,
An' lea'e us nought but grief an' pain,
For promised joy."

Allow me to give you the Price translation:

Ooooops!!!

I was about to have an awakening.
Let me explain. In my neighborhood there are no running trails, however there are good streets and areas to run and walk. Oh, before we continue I should clarify what I mean by "running", at least for me: When I was a

kid I felt like I could run at full tilt and never get tired. Now, well, not so much. Now, between just you and I of course, running has become a fast walk. Don't get me wrong I do wind sprints, but they're getting shorter.
    Give me a second; I've got to catch my breath. This is where the line from Robert Burns comes into play: *"The best laid plans of mice and men go awry..."*
    Running in my neighborhood was great. The leaves of the trees were starting to fall and though the grass in many neighbors' lawns was turning brown, our lawn was still green. Admittedly, not because of anything I had done; I've just got a really great lawn guy.
    Anyway, as I left the neighborhood, the shelter of the houses and crossed the main street, I felt great. As I make my turn about half way through my self-imposed five mile run, I discover something I had completely ignored. Up to this point the breeze had been to my back and now as I turned the corner it's directly in my face. **I'm running against the wind.**
    Once again Robert Burns: "The best laid plans of mice and men go awry... *And leave us nought but grief and pain... For promised joy..."* It's no longer a pleasurable run, it's a battle... its war... it's *"man I hope I can finish."* This run is going to be *"Nought but grief and pain."* Churchill was correct: "Victory is paid for in sweat, courage and preparation."
Finis Coranat Opus, *"The outcome crowns the victory."*
    I shall never forget reading about John Stephen Akhwari of Tanzania, Africa running in the Marathon of the Olympic Games in Mexico City, October 1968. Dur-

ing the marathon, John fell and injured his leg. He did, however, complete the race.

He was the last man to cross the finish line an hour after the rest have crossed the line. When ask by reporters why he
did not quit he responded: *"My country did not send me 5000 miles to start a race, they sent me 5000 miles to finish the race."*

Sometimes all we seem to have left to finish the course is as Winston Churchill put it when his country was facing what seemed to be insurmountable circumstances: *"I have nothing to offer but blood, toil, tears, and sweat.... You ask, what is our policy? I will say: It is to wage war, by sea, land, and air, with all our might and **with all the strength God can give us.... You ask, what is our aim? I can answer in one word: It is Victory.**"*

The Apostles Paul tells us:

*…let us run with **patience** the race that is set before us.*
Hebrews 12:1(KJV)

As Shakespeare in one of his opening soliloquies in Hamlet would have it, *"there's the rub"…* **patience** was not the answer I was looking for. At that moment with the wind in my face I wanted to take the words of the Apostle to Timothy:
*For **bodily exercise profiteth <u>little</u>:** but godliness is profitable unto all things…*
1 Timothy 4:8(KJV)

15

I wanted to be spiritual and forget this bodily exercise and **then he had to go and say:**

I therefore so run, not as uncertainly; so fight I, not as one that beateth the air.
1 Corinthians 9:26(KJV)

Oh! I know what he's referencing. The spiritual race and the running of that race has to do with things that have eternal significance. I just want to stop and change course because this running against the wind is getting harder.

Living in Oklahoma as I do, it seems that the wind never tires. There are moments that the wind seems to calm as if it is pausing to laugh at us and then as if to say "grab your hat" the wind hits you again. Running against the wind is tough.

I remember my wife, Paula, relating the story of her dad, Robert (Robby), just before his passing. He had for some time used a breathing aid. A week before his death, with his lungs filled with congestion and breathing difficult, he was diagnosed with stage-four cancer. During this time in the hospital, just days before he went home to be with the Lord, he had a vision. He gathered his family around and told them what he saw and felt. He related seeing people, family and friends he knew and that they recognized him also.

Then Robby said: *"I'm not afraid. I could run. I could breathe and I didn't get tired."* Less than two days later, Robby finished his race.

But here, in this world you're going to get tired and run out of breath and there will be times when you're running against the wind.

Let's see if we can put this into some kind of perspective. Simply put, you breathe air into your lungs, the air or the oxygen crosses the respiratory membrane into the blood, into the lung capillaries, enters red blood cells and the red blood cells are carried throughout the body by the circulatory system. Okay, that seems to be fairly straight forward. However, now it gets just a little more intrinsic. There are 60 to 90 trillion cells in the human body and they all need air, oxygen. If you put the human cells back to back, they could go around the earth 4.5 times. And every one of those cells has a library inside it, called a nucleus, which contains the DNA Code. The DNA Code is the blueprint of life… everything about us is there… from our hair and eye color to personality traits. You add all this together, with this running against the wind and it's no wonder I'm tired in just the first block of my neighborhood. There's gotta be someplace where I can sit down… man am I exhausted.

No wonder biologists tell us that our cells die off every seven years and are replaced by new ones. They're exhausted!!! And if I keep running into this wind *I'm* going to need to be replaced.

Then I read that David says, not once but twice. First in **2 Samuel 22:30**: *"For by thee I have **run through a troop**: by my God have I **leaped over a wall**.* "And then again in **Psalm 18:29**: *"For by thee I have **run through a** *troop; and by my God have I **leaped over a wall**.*" By the way, you'll probably hear these scriptures again throughout this book. Why? Because you remember what you rehearse!

Okay, people, it's been my experience that it's tough enough to run against the wind, but to go through a troop and leap over a wall? It's going to take God and a whole lot of momentum. I just turned the corner and I can still see my house. With all this wind in my face, why am I still trying to fill my lungs? Maybe there's something else at work here. Maybe there's a lesson to be learned, knowledge to be understood?

I like Charlie Brown in the Peanuts comic strip. Charlie Brown is at the beach building a beautiful sandcastle. As he stands back to admire his work, it is suddenly consumed by a huge wave. Looking at the smooth mound of sand that had been his creation a moment before, he says, **"there must be a lesson here, but I don't know what it is."**

That's how I feel, but I think I'm going to get an answer that I may not like.

RULES FOR BEING HUMAN
1) You will learn lessons.
2) There are no mistakes… only lessons.
3) A lesson is repeated until it is learned.
4) If you don't learn the easy lessons, they get harder.
5) You'll know you've learned a lesson when your actions change.

Something's gotta give…

Day by Day
The Notre Dame Prayer Book for Students

Run by my side; live in my heartbeat
Give strength to my steps
As the cold surrounds, as the wind pushes me.
I know you surround me.
As the sun warms me, as the rain cleanses me,
I know you are touching me, challenging, me, loving me.
And so I give you this run.
Thank you for matching my stride.
Amen.

Chapter Two

RUNNING IN THE DARKNESS

Running in the dark, no matter how familiar you may be with the terrain, is always disconcerting to say the least, because the terrain can change in so many different ways. Weather can change the topography. Rain can wash a ditch across a dirt path and the ditch doesn't have to be big, to catch your foot and make you trip. A limb from a tree blown down across your path can create havoc. Sometimes it's called "not paying attention to your surroundings." I had a runner once tell me that one morning before the sun came up, while it was still dark, that he ran into a street sign. I remember once reading a sign in Southern CA that warned of mountain lions coming down out of the mountains. There are things that are nocturnal, human and animal. I tend to be more wary of the humans than the animals, though I must admit that many years ago while running a levy in Louisiana that I looked down from the levy and saw dogs at the bottom looking up at me and then start running towards me. It caused my heart to leap into my throat. The thing about it was that the closer they got to the top of the levy the more tired they became and eventually stopped as I ran back across the levy it became entertaining to watch them run after me and then stop, but that was daytime. *I didn't try that at night.*

Several years ago, I remember running in an unfamiliar area late in the evening, there seemed to be a heaviness in the night air making it hard to breath; the street lamps were the only light I had. As it is with me after a while, my mind began to wander. I don't use headphones generally because I like to be aware of my surroundings. However, after some time elapsed I began thinking of other things: messages to be researched, services to be held, schedules to be put on the calendar, notes to be written, friends to be called… etcetera, etcetera.

The next thing I knew I was falling. I had not paid any attention to that one slab on the concrete sidewalk that was higher than the rest. The roots of a tree between the sidewalk and the curb had grown under the slab and raised the sidewalk up enough for me to catch my foot and throw me off balance. As I fell, I had enough presence of mind to throw out my hands to break the fall.

This is going to hurt, I thought.

And you know what? I was right.

I didn't break anything, only the palms of my hands and knees were scraped and bloody. But come to think of it, the fall *did* break my run. The rest of the run was different. My pace was off. There was a slight limp and the heels of my hands and my knee caps were tender. The antiseptic was going to be rough to put on. The wounds would need to be cleaned.

Oh, and one more important thing… I wasn't going to forget where I tripped and fell. That would be indelibly printed on my memory banks. It would be "etched in stone," as it were. I can remember it to this very day.

It's the pace that matters. I think that's what the Apostle Paul had in mind when he said *"run with patience."* When you're running, you try to find a pace that's good uphill as well as downhill. There is a weariness that comes in your body that makes you feel like you can't pick up your feet. You begin to feel the weight in your legs, your feet begin to feel like lead and if one is not careful, you will stumble and *fall*. Getting back up and starting to move again when your body is saying "No way, I'm not moving" can be difficult. Just getting up, at times, seems to take the most effort.

I like the story of the two guys in the woods hiking when they come upon some bear tracks. As they climb the mountain following the tracks, they find carcasses that the bear hunted and tore apart. Finally, they come to a clearing and look up to see the bear running down the hill toward them. One guy says to the other, "We've got to get out of here; that bear is charging at us." As he turns to run, he notices his friend changing his hiking shoes and putting on his running shoes, to which he inquires of his friend: "What are you doing? You can't outrun that bear." In response, his friend says, "I don't have to outrun the bear... just you."

In considering all this talk about running, I have to ask myself: "How honest can I be, first to myself and then to you?" I have discovered that there are reasons we are running against the wind. Sometimes we are either running *to* something or *away* from something. I think I can put this in perspective for us.

No matter how hard you try to run from God, you can never outrun Him or out-distance Him. David illuminates this thought when he says:

¹O LORD, thou hast searched me, and known me.
² Thou knowest my downsitting and mine uprising, thou understandest my thought afar off.
³ Thou compassest my path and my lying down, and art acquainted with all my ways.
⁴ For there is not a word in my tongue, but, lo, O LORD, thou knowest it altogether.
⁵ Thou hast beset me behind and before, and laid thine hand upon me.
⁶ Such knowledge is too wonderful for me; it is high, I cannot attain unto it.
⁷ Whither shall I go from thy spirit? **or whither shall I flee from thy presence?**

Psalms 139:1-7

I recall after a life dismantling experience of going out for a run. Oh, I had run before, this time it was different.

I remember the hot summer afternoon wind in my face; there it is again… ***I'm running against the wind.*** I could feel my lungs crying for more oxygen. I could feel muscles in my legs tightening up, I could feel the heat coming up through my running shoes from the pavement: "I can't stop, I won't stop, I refuse to stop," I said to myself. "I've done this once already today."

If I run hard enough and long enough, when I fall asleep tonight, it won't be sleep at all; I'll just kind of pass out from exhaustion. I don't take drugs or any kind of artificial substances to help me sleep because somewhere along life's road, I would have to ask myself, *What am I avoiding?* It all seems like some kind of bad dream. And I don't want to dream or think; I just want it all to go away. But I can't run fast enough or far enough.

Bertrand Russell was correct when he said; ***"One's past is a gradually increasing weight."*** It will slow you down. Sometimes the past is so painful that it is easier to bear the pain of the past than to anticipate the pain of the future. The past makes the future so unbearable.

If we keep living and acknowledging our past failures, mistakes, ineptitudes, and sins of the past, it will eventually take away our uniqueness. If we do not allow Christ to rescue us from ourselves, our sins and failures, those sins and failures begin to control us and we become victims of our pasts and, consequently, develop a victim mentality. Remember: God never consults your past to determine your future. If anyone is dwelling on your past, it's you, not God. God is looking forward, way ahead of you.

One of the things that has always amazed me is how a small pebble in your shoe can bring you to a halt. A tiny pebble, not any bigger than the tip of a needle or match head, can bring a two hundred pound man to a halt. The pebble demands you stop and take off your shoe. ***"Oh! What a relief it is."*** But when it's all said and done, it's that ***running against the wind*** that I contend with that slows me down and sometimes stops me dead in my tracks.

If you don't know where you're going, any road will take you there.

Louis Carrol

Chapter Three

YOU CAN'T OUT RUN YOU

No matter how far or fast you run, when you're finished the mirror on the wall will remind you that all the sweat and labor doesn't take you far enough from the you on the inside.

The Old Testament prophet helps put this into perspective for us:

As if a man did flee from a lion, and a bear met him; or went into the house, and leaned his hand on the wall, and a serpent bit him.
Amos 5:19

You may get by but you'll never get away. There will always be a head on collision somewhere down the road. If we are not careful, we will become prisoners of our own philosophies. The <u>main</u> philosophy being the philosophy of avoidance.

Malcolm Muggeridge, working as a journalist in India, left his residence one evening to go to a nearby river for a swim. As he entered the water, he saw an Indian woman from the nearby village that had come to have her bath. Muggeridge impulsively felt the allurement of the moment and temptation stormed into his mind. He had lived with this kind of struggle for years but had somehow fought it off in honor of his commitment to wife, Kitty.

On this occasion, however, he wondered if he could cross the line of marital fidelity. He struggled just for a moment and then swam furiously toward the woman, trying to outdistance his conscience. His mind fed him the fantasy that stolen waters would be sweet and he swam the harder for it. Now he was just two or three feet away from her and as he emerged from the water, any emotion that may have gripped him paled in insignificance when compared with the devastation that shattered him as he looked at her. "She was old and hideous... and her skin was wrinkled and, worst of all, she was a leper... this creature grinned at me, showing a toothless mask." The experience left Muggeridge trembling and muttering under his breath, "What a dirty lecherous woman!" **But then the rude shock of it dawned upon him – it was not the woman who was lecherous; it was his own heart** (1).

[9] *The heart is deceitful above all things, and desperately wicked: who can know it?*
[10] *I the LORD search the heart...*

Jeremiah 17:9-10

You may be able to outrun a lot of things but you just can't out run *you*. God can chase you down and find you no matter how far you've tried to run or how deep you try to go. You can't outrun yourself or God.

Allow me to share a few lines from one of the most profound poems ever written, "The Hound of Heaven." It was penned by an Englishman named Frances Thompson

(1859-1907). Thompson was a genius, but he became a drug addict and was on the run for many years. The poem describes God as the persistent hound who, with loving feet, follows and follows until he catches up with this person who is trying to run and flee from him.

> I fled Him, down the nights and down the days;
> I fled Him, down the arches of the years;
> I fled Him, down the labyrinthine *(tangled, twisted)* ways
> Of my own mind;
> and in the midst of tears
> I hid from Him......
> From those strong Feet that followed, followed after.
>
> But with unhurrying chase,
> And unperturbed pace,
> Deliberate speed, majestic instancy,
> They beat--and a Voice beat,
> More instant than the Feet......

Even after I became a Christian, "I fled Him, down the nights and down the days; I fled Him, down the labyrinthine ways."

I remember praying: *"Lord give me a way, a plan"* and out of His mercy, He would. Then I would say, *"Thank you I can handle it from here,"* only to find out I couldn't handle it without Him. What I was really saying to God is what Frank Sinatra sang, *"I Did It My Way."* That's what I wanted, My Way.

To some degree I think the *Soren Kierkegaard* was right that *"The Sickness unto Death is Despair."*

Running from God instead of running to God will lead to despair. You cannot outrun someone who rides on the *"wings of the wind."*

*And **he** rode upon a cherub, and did fly: and **he** was seen upon the wings of the wind.*
2 Samuel 22:11

*And **he** rode upon a cherub, and did fly: yea, **he** did fly upon the wings of the wind.*
Psalms 18:10

*...who maketh the clouds **his** chariot: **who** walketh upon the wings of the wind;*
Psalms 104:3

Run if you will and run if you can, but you will never outrun the wind. It will engulf you. You just can't outrun you because the *self* will always be there. In the bright light of day, there will be that feeling that something is chasing you. You will look back over your shoulder, just to see if someone is behind you. But you already know whose there. Like a haunting wind that seems to whistle through the trees. The kind of wind that somehow makes the house creak and groan. You can hear it in the chimney. It's an uneasy feeling. Those failures and mistakes and, oh yes, those sins that we don't talk about, that I don't talk about. I know they're forgiven, yet somehow they keep trying to return. They keep trying to chase me down and run over me. I ran with them so long. Then I tried to outrun them, but still they came back. I needed to find someone who could teach me how to leave them in the dust.

The book "Red Badge of Courage" contains a fictional portrait of a young soldier named Henry Fleming during an unnamed battle of the Civil War. Henry is an average farm boy from upstate New York, who dreams of the glory of battle that he has read about in school. The perpetual anticipation throws Henry into a bitter interior fight. He questions if he has the inner strength and courage to become a good soldier and is unsure whether or not it is in his realm of capability. He knows battle only through schoolbooks and soldiers' stories.

The Northern army is finally put on the move and marched across the river where they meet the Southern (Confederate) forces. The North seems to be winning, when the enemy charges again and Henry flees in the belief that his regiment will be overrun. He bitterly reproaches himself for running. In the end, Henry goes through many inner changes winning the internal war and bringing calm and peace (2).

That running on the inside will always challenge your staying power, your resilience. But stay the course and you will finish. There will always be that part of yourself that tries to stop or impede your progress, but keep on going.

I dislike the people who criticize and minimize others whose enterprise has made them rise above the people who criticize and minimize. Sometimes that person is me.

The Greeks had a race in their Olympic games that was unique. The winner was not the runner who finished first. It was the runner who finished with his torch still lit.

I want to run all the way with the flame of my torch still lit. May I keep the torch lit so that people can see Him who is the light of the world.

He will always be there when you fall or when you try to run away.

He was there all the time.

Run Forest run.

A Scottish atheist was sitting in his fishing boat when the mist began to roll up the moors. Suddenly, he was flung high in the air. As he reached the apex of his trajectory, he looked down and was staring into the mouth of the Loch Ness Monster.
"God save me!" He cried.
Suddenly, the clouds parted and a deep rumbling voice asked, *"Why should I save you, you don't believe in me?"*
To which the atheist replied, "A few minutes ago I didn't believe in the Loch Ness Monster, either."

Chapter Four

RUNNING WITH THE HORSES

If thou hast run with the footmen, and they have wearied thee, then how canst thou contend with horses? and if in the land of peace, wherein thou trustedst, they wearied thee, then how wilt thou do in the swelling of Jordan?
Jeremiah 12:5

    Horses… many times in the Bible represent warfare. Runners know that at the beginning of learning to run, there's a warfare that starts, which you will continue to fight always on some level. You will fight in your body, your mind, your emotions, and your spirit. You will be tempted to quit.

I remember running with other people and it always seemed like I was running with someone who was always faster, stronger, could talk at the same time and never run out of breath. It was always disparaging to be running only to see somebody younger or older run past you. Running with the footmen is tough enough, but running with the horses…. I'm going to have to think this through.

I've lived long enough to find out life is a warfare on some level all the time. You're not always going to be happy, satisfied, content with everything around you, and then there are the really hard things.

    Moses understood this running against wind, this dealing with the hard things that slow you down.

...and the cause that is too hard for you, bring it unto me, and I will hear it.

Deuteronomy 1:17

Moses is saying to the people: you're going to run into things that are hard for you to deal with. Its ok, He says, bring it to me. I'll help.

There are things in life that we feel are spiritually, intellectually, and emotionally too difficult to deal with. They are charged with such synergy, with such a collective force that they paralyze us and seem to render us incapable of response. We have an intellectual and emotional meltdown. We're exhausted and every breath is war. It's called fear. There are two acronyms for the word **FEAR**. **F**alse **E**vidence **A**ppearing **R**eal or **F**orget **E**verything **A**nd **R**un...

I heard about a newly appointed public servant who was setting himself up in his new office. As he sat at his desk for the first time, he discovered that his predecessor had left him three envelopes along with instructions that they should be **opened only in times of distress.**

Before long, the man was in trouble with the press, **so he decided to open the first envelope.** The note said, **"Blame your predecessor,"** So that's what he did. For a while things went smoothly.

But a few months later, he was in trouble again, so he opened the second envelope. The note said, **"Reorganize."** So that's what he did. That bought him more time.

But because **he had never really resolved any of the issues** that were causing him problems, he ended up in trouble again, and this time it was even greater than before. In desperation, he opened the last envelope. The note inside read, **"Prepare three envelopes."**

Sometimes we just want someone who we can run to with the hard things. There are some things that friends and family can fix, or at least that's what we think. The reality is, all they can really do is provide a temporary fix, maybe buy you a little time or perhaps bail you out. Eventually that won't work.

Moses gives us hope because God says to him:

If there arise ***a matter too hard for thee in judgment... get thee up into the place which the LORD thy God shall choose.***
Deuteronomy 17:8

There is a place you can go where God can answer the tough questions. This is a place where God will meet you.

Running with the horses means coming to grips with life and there are three life phases that I would like to address.

One is the phase of ***HETERONOMY***: rule by the laws made by another or an external source, such as parents, school, or governments who make laws.

This is usually okay until we discover the next phase: the phase of ***AUTONOMY***. This is self-rule, self-law.

We begin to think we are really in charge. Our human self rebels against the rule imposed by others in the *HETERONOMOUS phase* of our lives. But when *AUTONOMY* begins to break down and begins to fail we tend to want to go back to some kind of *HETERONOMOUS phase*, some kind of rule that will guarantee us security or relief. Many times it's drugs, alcohol, or even the government. At that point we're not looking for freedom, but security.

It is here in the third phase that the running, the war really takes place. It is the phase of **THEONOMY, RULE BY GOD**.

It is a gift…it is something you experience…you receive it. Jesus said:

Marvel not that I said unto thee, Ye must be born again.
John 3:7(KJV)

And the Apostle Peter reiterates this point and drives it home.

Being born again, not of corruptible seed, but of incorruptible, by the word of God, which liveth and abideth for ever.
1 Peter 1:23(KJV)

What do we do when we're running against the wind and trying to keep up with the horses? What do we do when it's not just battle fatigue we're dealing with but that constant badgering, berating of the enemy? The belittling, the condemnation, the incessant accusations?

Daniel gives us an insight speaking of our adversary. *"And he shall speak great words against the most High, and shall **wear out** the saints of the most High"* **(Daniel 7:25 KJV).**

In the Old Testament the term, **wear out** means **to fatigue mentally and emotionally. The enemy wants to wear you out.**

Jeremiah answers the question about bringing the hard things to God and it also helps us with our running.

*Ah Lord GOD! behold, thou hast made the heaven and the earth by thy great power and stretched out arm, and **there is nothing too hard for thee***
Jeremiah 32:17 KJV

In February of 2007, three runners put their hands down in the Red Sea to signify they had finished 111 days of running that had taken them through 6 countries and 4300 miles. They ran the equivalent of two marathons a day. In less than 4 months they had run across the world's largest desert, the Sahara and through 6 countries. The journey is one of extremes. Throughout the run, the runners dealt with tendinitis, cramping and knee injuries. Running through turbulent conditions, the relentless sun can push temperatures above 100 degrees Fahrenheit during the day, but at night it sometimes dips below freezing. Strong winds can abruptly send sand swooping in every direction, making it difficult to see and breathe.

Many times in the struggle of life's race, it's about making the effort of putting one foot in front of the other. Sometimes it's he that endures to the end.

Several years ago I was staying at a friend's house. In the evening I would go for a run and watch the sun go down behind the mountains and feel the temperature change as the sun would set.

About the same time that I would head out for my run, a man on a bicycle would ride his bike past the entrance where was I staying every day. As was my regimen, I would take time to stretch and watch as he would ride by me several times before I left the complex. As I made my way along the running path, I thought how strange it was that this man never left the community. He was not able to see the mountains or the flowers along the trail or meet with the other people who were either running, walking, or riding their bikes. For him the scenery never changed. Perhaps something bad had happened to him on some occasion outside the walls. I'm sure he felt safer and felt that he had better security. But the scenery just never changed.

It may not be a great analogy, but it spoke volumes to me. I was glad I was outside the wall. The trail was always different, the birds, the people, the sunset. Ahhh Life! Life is always better outside the walls. If you stay in those confining spaces nothing changes.

Jesus was always outside of the proverbial wall.

Outside the holy precincts, outside what the status quo, outside of what the religious community expected. No one could ever charge Jesus with training an elite guard planning to take over an empire.

His followers were **not trained** to kill others, only to die to self. They were trained to love their enemies and pray for those who despitefully use them. This is outside the proverbial norm. Jesus says, *"if someone compels you to go a mile, go with him twain"* **(Matthew 5:41)**. This was a reference to the practice of "impressment" which, among other things, allowed a Roman soldier to conscript a Jewish native to carry his equipment for one Roman mile *(milion = 1,000 paces, about 1,611 yards or 1,473 metres)* no easy task considering a Roman soldier's backpack could weigh upwards of 100 pounds (45.4 kg). Jesus's point was that his followers must relinquish their individual "rights" in order to advance God's kingdom through self-sacrifice.

Now you can begin to run with the horses.

HAVE I STAYED TOO LONG AT THE FAIR

I wanted the music to play on forever
Have I stayed too long at the fair?
I wanted the clown to be constantly clever
Have I stayed too long at the fair?
I bought me blue ribbons to tie up my hair,
But I couldn't find anybody to care.
The merry-go-round is beginning to slow now,
Have I stayed too long at the fair?
I wanted to live in a carnival city,
with laughter and love everywhere.
I wanted my friends to be thrilling and witty,
I wanted somebody to care.
I found my blue ribbons all shiny and new,
But now I've discovered them no longer blue.
The merry-go-round is beginning to taunt me
Have I stayed too long at the fair?
There is nothing to win and no one to want me
Have I stayed too long at the fair?

Billy Barnes

Chapter Five

YOU CAN'T OUT RUN THE BULL

For potential trespassers of an Indiana farm a sign on a fence post reads, *"If you cross this field you better do it in 9.8 seconds. The bull can do it in 10 seconds."*

There is an event held in several countries, Spain, Portugal, Mexico, Peru and in the south of France called "The Running of The Bulls." It is a stretch that covers about a half mile, through a narrow cordoned off street. Every year, between 200 and 300 people are injured during the run. A major risk is runners falling and piling up on each other. In such cases, injuries come both from asphyxia, contusions, even death to those in the pile and from goring if the bulls crush into the pile. This is one sport you want to be out in front.

Bill Hillman, a 32-year-old Chicago-based journalist, is an expert on the event. He even co-authored a book subtitled "How to survive the bulls of Pamplona." But on July 3, 2014, just knowing about bull running, even knowing enough to write an instruction manual on bull running, wasn't enough. A 1,320 pound fighting bull named Brevito lagged behind the pack just before entering the city's bull ring at the end of a rain-slicked run in the annual festival.

At an inopportune time, Brevito gored Hillman in the right thigh and a 35-year-old Spanish man in the chest.

Both men's injuries were serious but not life-threatening (1).

Or how about the man that the Spanish police were looking for who took a dangerous selfie recently during the running of the bulls in Pamplona? The man was seen taking a picture of himself with his cell phone as three bulls charged up on him. One misstep and the man could have been trampled.

On Monday, in the last run of the festival, one of six bulls that broke away from the pack chased down and gored two men in their legs, lifting them right off the ground, European media reported. Local authorities passed a bylaw that year to clamp down on people using filming devices during the annual run at the San Fermin Festival.

Three people, all British citizens, have been fined so far, reported the Spanish news website, "The Local." One man reportedly tried to film the bull run with a drone. If Mr. Selfie is caught he could face a fine of thousands of dollars. The Local reported that Spanish public TV filmed him taking the *selfie*. Pictures of the man circulated on Spanish social media with a hashtag that means "the idiot with the mobile" (2).

Many of us spend time trying to outrun something like our past and in so doing we open a quarrel between the past and the present, and find that we have lost the future.

We should remember as a wise man once said that **"The past teaches us, the present tests us and the future rewards us."** We must see the past as a teacher, not a master. See the present as a launching pad, not a prison.

So stop, don't disdain the past, don't disassemble the present and don't disallow the future.

We tend to worry about things, events and people in our past with which we tend to get bound by all the yesterdays of our lives. To untie your future, you got to tie up your past.

In every event, every circumstance, every condition, and every environment, there is human involvement. That's when you need to remember that there was a point in life when you began to realize:

Who matters.
Who never did.
Who won't.
And who always will.

So don't worry about people from your past, there's a reason they didn't make it to your future.

You can't change your past but with God's help you can get a future out of your past.

You can't con God, though you can con yourself. If you don't deal with the stuff of your past, the stuff will catch up to you.

You will feel like you are on the horns of a dilemma, between the devil and the deep blue sea, between a hard place and a rock. I think you get my drift, my meaning.

You just can't outrun the bull.

Ravi Zacharias tells of a story on the front page of a well-known international newspaper. It's the story of a truck driver in Italy who habitually visited brothels when he was on the road.

On one occasion, an associate told him about the best brothel he had been to and whom he should ask for to receive the best service. He decided to follow up on the recommendation even though he was so close to home. When he arrived at the brothel, he asked for the services of that particular prostitute and awaited her arrival. To his utter shock and anger, when the woman walked into the room he discovered she was his wife.

He was enraged, realizing that while he had been on the road his wife had been making a living through prostitution. Totally out of control, he grabbed her and would have killed her had he not been restrained.

Ravi makes this astute observation: *"I could not help shaking my head in utter disbelief as I read this story. Here was a man completely untroubled by his own duplicitous and debauched lifestyle. Yet when the tables were turned on him, he could not accept the horror of being a victim of his own philosophy"* (3).

Be sure your sin will find you out.
Numbers 32:23 (KJV)

Rosie Ruiz Vivas was declared the winner in the female category for the 84th Boston Marathon in 1980, only to have her title stripped after it was discovered that she had not run the entire course.

Running in and for the Kingdom of God isn't about fame or fortune. It's about character.

[1]LORD, who shall abide in thy tabernacle? who shall dwell in thy holy hill? [2]He that walketh uprightly (integrity)...
Psalms 15:1-2 (KJV)

Choices can be made in a moment and can reach far into your future, shaping your destiny.

It has been observed that *"Our lives are like icebergs. Only 15 percent is visible; that's reputation. The rest, our character, rests below the surface, hidden."*

Reputation is what people think of you because of what you appear to be; ***character*** is what both you and God know that you are. Outer charisma never substitutes for inner character. Follow character, not charisma. One is internal, the other external. The first is eternal, the latter temporary. Talent can be acquired and developed a lot quicker than character can be established.

William Hersey Davis (1887-1950) professor of New Testament interpretation at Southern Baptist Theological Seminary in Louisville, Kentucky from 1920 to 1948 wrote a piece on *The Difference Between Character and Reputation*. He states:

"Reputation is what you are supposed to be; **Character is what you are.** *Reputation is the photograph;* **Character is the face.** *Reputation comes over one from without;* **Character grows up from within.***"*

John Wooden, the legendary basketball coach of UCLA with four undefeated seasons of 30-0 and 19 conference championships, wrote in his autobiography of a lifetime with collegiate athletes: *"You should care more about your character than your reputation. Character is what you really are. Your reputation is only what people think about you."*

The ancient Greeks used the word "character" to describe the indelible mark left by a chisel after the powerful strike of the hammer. That's what character is, the indelible mark in a man or woman, true to the core.

Sometime ago I read about the great battle that rages inside us. One side is the soaring eagle. Everything the eagle stands for is good and true and beautiful, and it soars above the clouds. The other side is the howling wolf. And that raging howling wolf represents the worst that's in me. He eats upon my downfalls and justifies himself by his presence in the pack.

Who wins this great battle?

The one I feed.

I know what you're thinking. You're thinking I can't outrun all of this.

Remember the four-minute mile? People had been trying to achieve it since the days of ancient Greece. In fact, folklore had it that the Greeks had lions chase the runners, thinking that would make them run faster. They also tried drinking tiger's milk—not the stuff you get down at the health food store, but the real thing. Nothing they tried worked. So they decided it was impossible for a person to run a mile in four minutes or less. And for over a thousand years everyone believed it. Our bone structure is all wrong. Wind resistance is too great. We have inadequate lung power. There were a million reasons.

Then one man, one single human being, proved that the doctors, the trainers, the athletes, and the millions of runners before him, who tried and failed, were all wrong. And, miracle of miracles, the year after ***Roger Bannister a British runner broke the four-minute mile (3:59.4 on May 6, 1954),*** **thirty-seven other runners broke the four-minute mile.** The **year after that three hundred runners broke the four-minute mile.**

And a few years ago in a single race in New York, thirteen out of thirteen runners broke the four-minute mile.

In other words, a few decades ago the runner who finished dead last in the New York race would have been regarded as having accomplished the impossible. What happened? There were no great breakthroughs in training. No one discovered how to control wind resistance. Human bone structure and physiology didn't suddenly improve. But human attitudes did (4).

Years ago I remember going for a run in Brantford, Ontario. The city was laid out somewhat like an old wagon wheel. I started my run from my hotel not realizing the city's layout. I was thinking that all the streets were in a square pattern. I thought I could run one way on this street and back on another just a block over. However, the further I went out on my run, other streets came between the street I was on and the street I thought was just a block over. I learned a valuable lesson.

You can create your own maze and become disoriented and be like a dog chasing his tale. Fortunately, I had the good sense to ask for help and direction. I tried to put on a mask that would disguise my angst but my question betrayed me: *"I'm lost. Can you help me?"*

He knows where I am.

I'm not lost to Him.

I know my Redeemer Liveth.

Every morning in Africa, a gazelle wakes up. It knows that it must run faster than the fastest lion or it will be killed. Every morning a lion wakes up. It knows that it must outrun the slowest gazelle or it will starve to death. It doesn't matter whether you are a lion or a gazelle: When the sun comes up, you had better be running.

Chapter Six

RUNNING A FEVER

[19] *Then said Ahimaaz the son of Zadok, Let me now run, and bear the king tidings, how that the LORD hath avenged him of his enemies.*
[20] *And Joab said unto him, Thou shalt not bear tidings this day, but thou shalt bear tidings another day: but this day thou shalt bear no tidings, because the king's son is dead.*
[21] *Then said Joab to Cushi, Go tell the king what thou hast seen. And Cushi bowed himself unto Joab, and ran.*
[22] *Then said Ahimaaz the son of Zadok yet again to Joab, But howsoever, let me, I pray thee, also run after Cushi. And Joab said,* **Wherefore wilt thou run, my son, seeing that thou hast no tidings ready?**
[23] *But howsoever, said he, let me run. And he said unto him, Run.* **Then Ahimaaz ran by the way of the plain, and overran Cushi.**
[24] *And David sat between the two gates: and the watchman went up to the roof over the gate unto the wall, and lifted up his eyes, and looked, and behold a man running alone.*
[25] *And the watchman cried, and told the king. And the king said, If he be alone, there is tidings in his mouth. And he came apace, and drew near.*
[26] *And the watchman saw another man running: and the watchman called unto the porter, and said, Be-*

hold another man running alone. And the king said, He also bringeth tidings.

²⁷And the watchman said, Me thinketh the running of the foremost is like the running of Ahimaaz the son of Zadok. And the king said, He is a good man, and cometh with good tidings. ²⁸And Ahimaaz called, and said unto the king, All is well. And he fell down to the earth upon his face before the king, and said, Blessed be the LORD thy God, which hath delivered up the men that lifted up their hand against my lord the king.

²⁹And the king said, Is the young man Absalom safe? And Ahimaaz answered, When Joab sent the king's servant, and me thy servant, I saw a great tumult, but I knew not what it was.

2 Samuel 18:19-29(KJV)

As a Christian we have a message that must be delivered. God runs the universe and He sent Jesus with a message. Jesus came to lay down His life and picked up the cross so we could win this race in our lives. Athletes understand that sacrifices must be made in order to take up the disciplines and challenges to finish the course.

When you forget the **why in your endeavor**, you will tend to pick up artificial stimuli to help you, and in turn you create an artificial life.

Running without purpose is pointless and running without passion is powerless.

Ahimaaz was a good runner. He outran Cushi because he took the short cut. He ran, but he didn't have the message. He didn't have firsthand knowledge. He didn't know what was important to the king. He didn't have the information; he just saw a lot of action and got the *Fever to Run.*

Just recently I was on a run, but because the trail was covered with loose rock due the recent weather, I decided to turn the run into hike. As I was going, I saw what seemed to be an easier path only to find it more difficult. After traversing this way and that, I finally found my way back to the main path. After a few moments of collecting my thoughts, I came to the conclusion that I didn't have the right information and could have avoided all the brush and the low limbs of the trees if I had only ask someone.

I must insert here that I don't want to say I was lost on this hike, I just prefer to say what Daniel Boone once said to Chester Harding, the only artist to paint a life portrait of the frontiersman: *"I can't say as ever I was lost, but I was bewildered once for three days!"*

I was just bewildered. OK! I know I just didn't have the right information.

Running A Fever is to want something without the correct information which proves the old adage "buyer beware."

Sometime ago in the purchase of Rolls-Royce Motor Cars, Volkswagen and BMW battled each other to purchase Rolls Royce from Vickers PLC. Volkswagen won the battle, paying $780 million for the luxury automaking company. After the purchase was finalized, the buyers made a shocking discovery. Volkswagen owned the company, but not the rights to the name Rolls Royce, which is synonymous with luxury cars around the world. The license for the name, it turned out, belonged to another company: Rolls-Royce PLC, an aerospace company. Even, worse, Rolls-Royce PLC had ties to BMW. Guess who received permission to use the name? BMW not Volkswagen. And it all happened because of poor information gathering (1).

Many times we discover in all our moving around that we have to wait. Sometimes, we need to wait. When I run, I dislike waiting at stop lights. But I'm not faster than a three thousand pound car doing fifty miles an hour.

Several months ago Paula and I were in Florida during the NASCAR Coke 400 race in July. We had planned our schedule so we would be at our ministry destination and miss the traffic in Daytona. But the rains came and the race was suspended on Saturday and continued on that Sunday at 11 AM.

Needless to say everyone waited trying to get to church on Sunday. Friends who had come some distance told of having to wait thirty minutes just to go four miles.

It seems with all of our running there are times, we will have to wait. When you want to run, waiting isn't easy. It has been said that we will spend at least three years of our lives waiting. I told my wife the other day I was running *(in my car)* to the store only to have to wait in line when I got there.

We run to the doctor's office only to sit in the waiting room; we run to the car only to wait stuck in traffic; hurry to lunch just to wait in line, we run to the store just to wait in line. Waiting. It seems with all of our running, we're still having to wait quite a lot.

When you're running, you have to press on to get your second wind. This second wind is what helps you finish.

Wait on the LORD: *be of good courage, and* ***he shall strengthen thine heart:*** *wait, I say, on the LORD.*
Psalms 27:14(KJV)

But ***they that wait upon the LORD shall renew*** *their strength; they shall mount up with wings as eagles;* ***they shall run, and not be weary;*** *and they shall walk, and not faint.*
Isaiah 40:31(KJV)

We're running to catch the train or the bus or the plane. Our computers, iPads, and iPhones are running fast but not fast enough, and our anxiety is growing exponentially. Some of us are already praying the **"Anxiety Prayer"**:

God grant me anxiety and worry,
So that I can fret about things just out of my reach,
And neglect the things you've given me.

I pray I would learn to confuse what's mine
to do and what's yours.
Allow me to live in the future; ignoring the present
and its treasure.
You know I won't enjoy anything till
I have everything I want.
Please remove all my hardships so I can finally have
peace.
I pray that everyone will see it my way
and everything will go my way.
We've been over this before God—you know things
won't work out unless you do it my way;
unless you listen to me carefully.
You know I'm miserable and probably always will be.
If anybody will be unhappy in the next life,
it'll probably be me.
I knew it—worry forever, it's my lot.

Sometimes we're running in such a fever that we run past our hope, our miracle, our healing.
I recall after a painful experience in my life running in a fever to forget. I tried to outrun the pain. I was in Sanford, NC staying with a Pastor. At that time I was running two or three times a day. On this occasion I woke up about 3 AM to go for a run. I put on my running gear, came down stairs and began to lace up my running shoes only to be startled by the Pastor who had been waiting for me. He told me that during the night the Lord spoke to him and gave him a message for me. The Pastor had been

up for a long time to catch me before I ran. He announced to me that the Lord said to tell me: "Stop running." I knew what he meant. It wasn't about physical running, it was about what I was running from. Though I understood and knew it was truth, I had run for so long that I just couldn't stop. I thanked him and headed out the door. The good news is with God's help I overcame.
*...**let us lay aside every weight**, and the **sin** which doth so easily beset us...*
Hebrews 12:1(KJV)

I recall that when I was in the Army at Fort Polk, Louisiana running at port arms with a full backpack. I can't speak for anyone else but it never seemed to get easier. Ah... but the moment you could sling your weapon and backpack down... "Oh! What a relief it is."

Today when I run, I try to find the lightest clothing and shoes to wear. Oh, I take my cell phone but sometimes it seems to get heavy.

The Apostle Paul understood weight.

The weight that he talks about means *"hindrance."* The sin he talks about is *"offence."* Sin turns our focus into condemnation and guilt. Condemnation and guilt always become a weight and slow us down.

Sin distracts us.

What distracts us ... detaches us.

What detaches us ... disables us.

What disables us ... destroys us.

Wherefore seeing we also are compassed about with so great a cloud of witnesses…
Hebrews 12:1(KJV)

This cloud of witnesses were ***ex-runners*** who had already completed the course and now they are spectators.

My dad would say to me when something got tough: *"pull yourself up by your bootstraps and get going."*

Someone has already been down this road. There's a whole crowd of witnesses watching you and cheering you on. They're telling you: "We've been where you are, you can finish, we're pulling for you. Don't stop. Keep moving. We did it. You can do it."

From the portals of glory, if we could see it, the great Apostle Paul would be shouting down: "Remember what I said!!!"

[24] *Know ye not that they which run in a race run all, but one receiveth the prize? So run, that ye may obtain.*
[25] *And every man that striveth for the mastery is temperate in all things. Now they do it to obtain a corruptible crown; but we an incorruptible.*
[26] ***I therefore so run**…*
1 Corinthians 9:24-26(KJV)

This is one race you can win. You're not a loser here, you're a winner. That's why Paul says:

*...let us **run with patience** the race that is set before us...*
Hebrews 12:1(KJV)

One of the difficult things to do is to find the right pace. Stay steady.

Paul says it's going to take some endurance, but with Christ you can make it. You can finish.

⁷... I have finished my course...
⁸...there is laid up for me a crown of righteousness, which the Lord, the righteous judge, shall give me at that day: and not to me only, but unto all them...
2 Timothy 4:7-8(KJV)

Eric Liddell *(whose life the movie "Chariots of Fire" was based on)* took a difficult stand in his bid to win the gold medal in the 1924 Olympics in Paris. He had trained hard for the **200 meters**, but just days before the event, he found out that the heats were on a Sunday. It was against Liddell's conviction to run on the Lord's Day. So he told his coach he was pulling out of the event.

The entire coaching staff and the management tried to talk him out of it and even considered dropping him altogether. They finally decided that if they were successful in persuading him to set aside his deep convictions, it would change who he was and affect how he ran. So they let him run in the **400-meter race, an event that was not his primary strength.**

The moment came and he was on the track for the race.

Just before they took to their marks, **Jackson Schulz, the American runner, walked over to Eric and handed him a piece of paper. Eric looked at the paper and saw the words from 1 Samuel 2:30:** *"Them that honour me I will honour, says the Lord."*

Eric Liddell clutched that piece of paper and ran the race of his life. He won the gold and showed the world what true winning is all about.

OK, now take a deep breath. There's a hill coming up that you're about to climb. Now you can.

The Runner's Prayer

Lord, Watch over me today as I run.
This is the day and this is the time for the race.
Watch over my body.
Keep it free from injury.
Watch over my mind.
May I listen to the signals from within
as I enjoy the scenes from without.
Watch over my spirit.
Watch over my competitors.
Remind us that we all are struggling equally.
Lord,
Let me win.
Not by coming in ahead of my friends,
but by beating myself.
Let it be an inner win.
A battle won over me.
And may I say at the end,
"I have fought a good fight.
I have finished the race.
I have kept the faith."

Adapted from The Ultrarunner's Prayer by Carolyn Erdman & Jay Hodde

Chapter Seven

RUNNING INJURED

There's an old Irish Prayer that goes like this:

May those who love us, love us;
And those who don't love us
May God turn their hearts;
And if He doesn't turn their hearts
May He turn their ankles,
So we'll know them by their limping.

For a runner, injuries are plentiful: everything from a twisted ankle to stress fractures occur. I know about twisted ankles, knee problems, and ligament pulls. All are painful and take time to heal.
 I've read how stress can affect us and our concentration, and when you run you need to concentrate.

This was given to me for stress. It's called the stress diet.

THE STRESS DIET
This diet is designed to help you cope with the stress that builds up during the day.

BREAKFAST
1 grapfruit

1 slice whole wheat toast
8 oz. skim milk

LUNCH
4 oz. lean broiled chicken breast
1 cup steamed spinach
1 cup herb tea
1 Oreo cookie

MID-AFTERNOON SNACK
The rest of Oreos in the package
2 pints Rocky Road ice cream, with nuts, cherries and whipped cream, and topped with 1 jar hot fudge sauce

DINNER
2 loaves garlic bread
4 cans or 1 large pitcher Coke
1 large sausage, mushroom and cheese pizza
3 Snicker bars

EVENING SNACK
Entire frozen Sara Lee cheesecake (eaten directly from freezer)

OTHER HELPFUL TIPS:
If you eat something and no one sees you eat it, it has no calories.
Anything consumed while standing has no calories. This is due to gravity and the density of the caloric mass.

Anything consumed from someone else's plate has no calories since the calories rightfully belong to the other person and will cling to his/her plate. (We ALL know how calories like to cling!)

REMEMBER: STRESSED SPELLED BACKWARDS IS DESSERTS.

Joseph Parker, a nineteenth century preacher, said that if you preach to hurting hearts, you will never want for a congregation; there is one in every pew. There will always be broken and hurting people around us.

Phillip Yancey in book "Grace Notes" tells a story that moves me every time I think of it.

During one of he and his wife's trips to Nepal, a therapist gave he and his wife, Janet, a tour of the Green Pastures Hospital, which specializes in leprosy rehabilitation. He writes:

"As we walked along an outdoor corridor, I noticed in a courtyard one of the ugliest human beings I have ever seen. Her hands were bandaged in gauze and she had deformed stumps for feet, her nose had shrunken away so that looking at her I could see into her sinus cavity. Her eyes mottled and covered with callus, let in no light; she was totally blind. Scars covered patches of skin on her arms.

This creature crawled to the very edge of the walkway, pulling herself along the ground by planting her elbow and dragging her body. Without hesitation my wife bent and put her arm around the woman, who rested her head against Janet's shoulder and began singing a song in Nepali, a tune that we all instantly recognized: 'Jesus Loves Me.'"

In our world today people are so busy with the things of life that they forget that people are not inanimate objects.

When Edmond Hillary and his native guide, Tenzing, made their historic climb of Mt. Everest, coming down from the peak, Hillary suddenly lost his footing. Tenzing held the line taut and kept them both from falling by digging his ax into the ice. Later Tenzing refused any special credit for saving Hillary's life. As he put it, "Mountain climbers always help each other."

Runners help each other.

For by thee I have run *through a troop; and* ***by my God*** *have I leaped over a wall.*
Psalms 18:29(KJV)

Runners know that sometimes you can run through pain and sometimes pain will stop you in your tracks. I remember a runner talking about getting older and going for a jog. He recalls that when he was a younger athlete, running was easier, but now that he's older, jogging is different.

He relays as he jogged he had a slight pain in the knee but he rubbed it and kept going, but then the pain came back with more intensity and he had to stop. Finally his pain shouted so loudly that he had to sit down on a curb. Then, as he put it, his knee said 'thank you very much'.

The exchange between him and his painful knee is both humorous and somewhat revealing.

Life is full of pain. Neil Simon observed: *"If you can go through life without experiencing pain you probably haven't been born yet"* (1).

In 2004, NBC News ran an article on a disease called **congenital insensitivity to pain** (CIP), also known as **congenital analgesia**. It is a rare condition in which a person cannot feel (and has never felt) physical pain. The disease, according to medical analysis, is at this point untreatable. This rare disease is only shared by a few in the world; less than one hundred are documented. Imagine not knowing when you have scalded your mouth on a hot meal or bit your tongue so badly that it bled. Imagine your child reaching out for the flickering light of a candle and not having the pain of burned fingers to reinforce your scolding plea not to play with fire. Pain is necessary. Regardless of how slight or severe, pain is the body's signal for danger.

Many like me have tried to navigate through life to avoid feeling the kind of pain that numbs you emotionally, intellectually, and spiritually. The kind of pain that blocks you from having a genuinely full and productive life.

The problem is that we don't just try to move through life without feeling pain, we start ***RUNNING INJURED*** through life blindly. We don't see others who are wounded, limping through life with pain. Our pain blinds us to those around us. Soon we all discover that we are not impervious to life's pain.

CS Lewis in the pages of "A Grief Observed" poignantly describes watching his wife lose her battle with cancer and wrestling with God through the pain. He is then writing as a man who bitterly, tortuously, and intimately knows what he knows to be true of God and evil, suffering and Christ though his soul is breaking. Lewis writes, *"Your bid for God or no God, for a good God or the Cosmic Sadist, for eternal life or nonentity, will not be serious if nothing much is staked on it. And you will never discover how serious it was until the stakes are raised horribly high."* He continues, *"Nothing will shake a man - <u>or at any rate a man like me</u> - out of his merely verbal thinking and his merely notional beliefs. He has to be knocked silly before he comes to his senses. Only torture will bring out the truth. Only under torture does he ever discover himself"* (2).

I purposely underlined the phrase in CS Lewis' statement *"<u>or at any rate a man like me</u>"* for those among us who feel exempt from pain because they have arrived at such a spiritual place of nirvana, that they are so holy they don't leave tracks. Yet that would put one on a plane that Christ didn't walk on. Christ left His footprints and fingerprints everywhere He went.

For unto you it is given in the behalf of Christ, not only to believe on him, but also to suffer for his sake;
Philippians 1:29(KJ

If we suffer, we shall also reign with him: if we deny him, he also will deny us.
2 Timothy 2:12(KJV)

Yea, and all that will live godly in Christ Jesus shall suffer persecution.
2 Timothy 3:12(KJV)

[24] By faith Moses, when he was come to years, refused to be called the son of Pharaoh's daughter; [25] Choosing rather to suffer affliction with the people of God, than to enjoy the pleasures of sin for a season.
Hebrews 11:24-25(KJV)

For what glory is it, if, when ye be buffeted for your faults, ye shall take it patiently? but if, when ye do well, and suffer for it, ye take it patiently, this is acceptable with God.
1 Peter 2:20(KJV)

But and if ye suffer for righteousness' sake, happy are ye: and be not afraid of their terror, neither be troubled.
1 Peter 3:14(KJV)

Yet if any man suffer as a Christian, let him not be ashamed; but let him glorify God on this behalf.
1 Peter 4:16(KJV)

David states in the Psalms without equivocation:

For by thee I have run through a troop; and by my God have I leaped over a wall.
Psalms 18:29(KJV)

David does not dismiss the fact that there will be troops against you and obstacles in our path, ***but run on anyway***. For by Him, through Christ, we can run through a troop. Even though we are injured with fragilities and failures, with wars within and without, with ineptitudes and inexperience, with mistakes and mismanagement, even with eyes and don't see and ears and don't hear… still with Him I can run through my weaknesses and leap over the ***snares*** and pitfalls that the enemy has laid out for me.

*Surely he shall deliver thee from the **snare** of the fowler, and from the noisome pestilence.*
Psalms 91:3(KJV)

*The wicked have laid a **snare** for me: yet I erred not from thy precepts.*
Psalms 119:110(KJV)

*Our soul is escaped as a bird out of the **snare** of the fowlers: the snare is broken, and we are escaped.*
Psalms 124:7(KJV)

*When my spirit was overwhelmed within me, **then thou knewest my path**...*
Psalms 142:3(KJV)

God knows the path that you're running on. You can't lose Him. The 11th century Rabi Judah Ha Levi stated: ***"I ran out to find my God and found him running after me."***

Thou wilt *show me the path* of life...
Psalms 16:11(KJV)

Teach me thy way, O LORD, and *lead me in a plain path*, because of mine enemies.
Psalms 27:11(KJV)

Thy word is a *lamp unto my feet, and a light unto my path.*
Psalms 119:105(KJV)

Eileen Cronin-Noe's life illustrates triumph over circumstances. She was born with only a portion of her upper right leg and her left leg has only a small underdeveloped calf below the knee. Her parents believed she was a gift from God. **Amniocentesis can't tell any parents what kind of child they will have. It can only tell what disability might exist in that child.**

As Eileen stated, "Amniocentesis could never have told my mother that I would have artistic talent, a high intellectual capacity, a sharp wit, and an outgoing personality."

Eileen tells of difficult experiences, especially the cruelty of other children as she grew up. But she walks tall with artificial legs. She grew up taking ballet lessons, playing softball, dating, and fully enjoying high school social life. As a young adult she graduated from college and moved on to receive a master's degree and begin doctoral studies.

She married and became a mother. Circumstances never tell the whole story of our lives. Most of our biographies are written from the values we hold and contain our responses to those circumstances (3).

Don't let your past dictate you future.

"RUN THROUGH THE TROOP AND LEAP OVER THE WALL."

JESUS LOVES ME THIS I KNOW…

RUN ON

'Still Running'

I been running for Jesus a mighty long time
and I'm still running
Running for Jesus a mighty long time
and I'm still running

Where ever you send me Lord I'll go
I'm still determined to reach my goal
I'm still running
99 and ½ won't do
Got to make 100 before I'm thru
Said I'm gonna run until He comes for me
I've got to see what the end is gonna be
Said I'm still
Still running

Dottie Peoples

Chapter Eight

RUN WITH THE WIND

Several years ago a Pastor friend of mine who enjoyed sailing invited me to accompany him sailing on a small lake. I agreed. So we rented a sail boat and set out on a wonderful day full of sunshine and a few beautiful clouds. At this point I should point out that I am not a sailor. I do, however, understand that with a sail boat wind is essential. Much to our good fortune we had a wonderful breeze.

So we set sail. My friend maneuvered the sail boat expertly. Though the sail boat wasn't very big, it was a most pleasurable time. There was leisurely conversation about one thing then another. We chatted about everything from sports to sermons we had ministered on or would be ministering.

Then it dawned on us after a period of time, that the wind had died down completely. The boat was small enough that we could have rowed to shore except for the fact we didn't have anything on board to row with.

Armed with this information and realizing the distance to shore was more than he or I could swim, my fine-tuned analytical mind begin to calculate the hourly cost of the sail boat. Oh brother! The wind had better kick in and pick up quick.

I watched my friend as he moved the sail this way and that way trying to find a bit of wind, but to no avail.

Then just as quickly as the wind had dissipated it returned. Now the wind was in our sails. I haven't been back on a sail boat since. I guess I should try it one more time as long as I know the wind will be with me.

Ah, but the wind felt good. I felt inspired. I wanted to sing, I wanted to fly. My mom used to sing: *"I'll fly away oh glory."*

*And **the hand of the LORD** was on Elijah; and he girded up his loins, and **ran** before Ahab to the entrance of Jezreel.*

1 Kings 18:46(KJV)

The distance from Mount Carmel to Jezreel was about seventeen miles. Jezreel was known as a city of chariots. It excelled in warfare because of its vast fleet of iron vehicles made for swift movement in battle.

Elijah had just called fire down from heaven. He told King Ahab to head home, that it was getting ready to rain. If a man who just called fire down from heaven is now saying it's going rain, then trust me, it's going to rain. And Ahab believed it.

From all that we can gather about Ahab and his wife, Jezebel, their arrogance and egos were enormous.

Ahab told his driver to bring the chariot around, and up pulls the finest chariot loaded with horse power. The best bred horse power that ego could find. Ahab probably told his driver as he grabbed the reins, "You can walk." I can see Ahab as he lays the whip to the horses. *Ignition on.* The horse power leaps into full throttle. The horses manes are flying, Ahab's eyes are watering from the wind. Nothing can stop him now or beat him. Except for one little thing.

Up on the Mount an old prophet is suddenly energized. Something explodes inside him. Elijah ties his coat around him and cinches up his belt and heads down the mountain, without a team of horses or a chariot to ride in. Something else is moving him, a different kind of propulsion.

He feels exhilarated, inspired, energized. He catches up with Ahab.

Ahab is doing his best to miss the rocks and stones in the old trail and not get off into the sand where he'd get stuck. He's almost down the mountain when he picks up something in his peripheral vision. It's startling. It can't be. In a moment's time, it's all revealed. Elijah runs in front of the horses all the way to Jezreel.

I've never had anything like that experience. I have, however, felt acceleration, a burst of adrenalin, a short burst of energy while I was running. It was brief. I felt like Mohamad Ali, "float like butterfly." Oh, what a rush. I can only imagine what Elijah felt. Ahab felt the wind in his face.

He was **running against the wind, but Elijah felt the wind at his back, carrying him along.**

It must have felt like he could hardly touch the ground with his feet.

*¹The **hand of the LORD** was upon me, and carried me out in the spirit of the LORD, and set me down in the midst of the valley which was full of bones,*
²And caused me to pass by them round about: and, behold, there were very many in the open valley; and, lo, they were very dry.
³And he said unto me, Son of man, can these bones live? And I answered, O Lord GOD, thou knowest.
⁴Again he said unto me, Prophesy upon these bones, and say unto them, O ye dry bones, hear the word of the LORD.
⁵Thus saith the Lord GOD unto these bones;
*Behold, **I will cause breath to enter into you**, and ye shall live:*
⁶And I will lay sinews upon you, and will bring up flesh upon you, and cover you with skin, and put breath in you, and ye shall live; and ye shall know that I am the LORD.

Ezekiel 37:1-6(KJV)

Here as well as **1 Kings 18:46** with Elijah the turn phrase is "The ***hand of the Lord was on***..." and then He says in verse (5)... ***I will cause breath to enter into you***...

There have been times that I've prayed to God to put His hand on me and help me, just a little more breath. We're all gonna need help.

The 1992 Olympics were in Barcelona and one event in particular received repeated telecasts. Derek Redman, a U.K. runner in the 400 meter race pulled a hamstring about 300 meters into the event. That is a painful injury and it would be nearly impossible to continue a race. But Derek did not quit. In a few moments an older man jumped from the stands, ran onto the track, and threw an arm around Derek. Together they finished the race long after all the other athletes. The crowd went wild for Derek. The TV camera operators followed every step of the painful ordeal. In the post-race interviews Derek Redman got more face time on worldwide television than the men who received the medals. Of course he was asked, "Who was the guy that helped you? Did you know him?"

"Yes, it was my father."

When we need help Abba, The Father, is there to put His arms around us and help us finish. I don't know about you but I'm breathing better already.

The word breathe for Ezekiel means "to cause to breathe" or "forcible respiration."

Remember earlier I told you of Robby's vision? He told his family, *"I could run. I could breathe and I didn't get tired."*

That story makes me breathe a little easier now.

When you're inspired, you can do things you never thought you could do, dream larger and begin to think outside the box.

Long before Paula's dad went home to be with our Lord and Savior, he had taken the road less traveled as we all should do. In 1915, Robert Frost wrote this poem;

THE ROAD NOT TAKEN
Two roads diverged in a yellow wood,
And sorry I could not travel both
And be one traveler, long I stood
And looked down one as far as I could
To where it bent in the undergrowth;
Then took the other, as just as fair,
And having perhaps the better claim,
Because it was grassy and wanted wear;
Though as for that the passing there
Had worn them really about the same,
And both that morning equally lay
In leaves no step had trodden black.
Oh, I kept the first for another day!
Yet knowing how way leads on to way,
I doubted if I should ever come back.
I shall be telling this with a sigh
Somewhere ages and ages hence:
Two roads diverged in a wood, and I-
I took the one less traveled by,
And that has made all the difference.

The *Via Dolorosa* for us will be the road less traveled. The human heart does not want to run that road. Crosses will have to be carried on this road. We will be our brother's keeper. Love our enemies. Pray for those who spitefully use us. Things will have to be crucified when running this road.

Excuse me for a moment while I take a deep breath.

Thank you Father. I can breathe now. I can run now. I can make it home.

An Irish Blessing
May the road rise to meet you,
May the wind be always at your back,
May the sun shine warm upon your face,
The rains fall soft upon your fields and,
Until we meet again,
May God hold you in the palm of His hand.

Chapter Nine

YOU DID RUN WELL

Ye did run well; who did hinder you that ye should not obey the truth?
Galatians 5:7(KJV)

It's rarely a what that hinders us. It's usually a who. And that who is usually me. I can talk myself into or out of doing something better than anyone else in the world. But then I'm left with all the questions.
 Did I miss my turn?
  Why this road and not some other road with less pain?
 Did I miss my cue?
 Why is it taking so long?
 Why do I feel out of sync and out of balance with life?
 If I'm a Christian, why is all this happening?
 Heading for Heaven is a bumpy road and I didn't expect it…but I'm on it now…what do I do?

 Keep on running.

 The adversary is more subtle than the rest of creatures. He knows how to turn me in on myself, especially while I'm running to and for the kingdom of Jesus Christ. *You'll never finish. You're too weak. You don't have enough strength. You're not smart enough. You're too big, too small, too fat, too skinny. You're the wrong col-*

or, you don't read the right books, you don't have the right education. **As a matter of fact you're more wrong than right in just about every area.**

The Peanuts comic strip puts it into perspective: Lucy puts her hands on her hips and says, "You Charlie Brown are a foul ball in the line drive of life! You're in the shadow of your own goal post! You are a miscue! You are three putts on the eighteenth green! You are a seven ten split in the tenth frame! You are a dropped rod and reel in the lake of life! You are a missed free throw, a shanked nine iron and a called third strike! Do you understand? Have I made myself clear?"

Yes, Lucy, you have made yourself perfectly clear.

This makes the Apostle Paul's writings even more important.

And let us not be weary in well doing: for in due season we shall reap, if we faint not.
Galatians 6:9(KJV)

Adversities do not make the man either weak or strong. They reveal what he is.
The poet W. H. Auden challenges us not to be afraid of adversities, astutely addressing the problem for most of us. "We would rather be ruined than changed. We would rather die in our dread than climb the cross of the moment and let our illusions die."

The dread of making life changes can be excruciatingly unbearable. I remember my dad saying that "changes are here to stay."
If we are not careful, we will become the masters of procrastination and invalid excuses.

"You did run well; who did hinder you…"

Some time ago I read a series of actual quotes taken from insurance accident forms.

- "The other car collided with mine without giving warn-ing of its intentions."

- "I collided with a stationary truck coming the other way."

- "The guy was all over the road; I had to swerve a number of times before I hit him."

- "I pulled away from the side of the road, glanced at my mother-in-law, and headed over the embankment."

- "In my attempt to kill a fly, I drove into a telephone pole."

- "I had been driving for forty years when I fell asleep at the wheel and had an accident."

"The pedestrian had no idea which direction to go, so I ran over him."
- "The telephone pole was approaching fast. I attempted to swerve out of its path when it struck my front end."
- "I was unable to stop in time and my car crashed into the other vehicle. The driver and passenger then left immediately for a vacation with injuries."

There's always an excuse not to start running. Church is boring, the pastor's message was too long and the worship and music was dull. You see how I slid in the spiritual aspect and connected it with running? Clever, huh? "You did run well; who did hinder you…"

   Watching Usain Bolt run and making it seem so effort-less is amazing. He is widely regarded as the fastest person ever; he is the first man to hold both the 100 meter and 200 meter world records since fully automatic time measurements became mandatory in 1977. However, Bolt is 30th on the list of the fast creatures on record. The white tail deer, warthogs, grizzly bears, and house cats are faster.
   An Arabian horse can run 60 miles, averaging 16 mph. Along with a certain natural ability, there's something else he has… "commitment" (1).
   W. H. Murray was a member of the Scottish team whose expeditions were the first to conquer several Himalayan Mountains. His remarks are imperative: **"Until one is committed there is hesitancy, the chance to draw back which creates ineffectiveness. In all acts**

of initiative there is one elementary truth, the ignorance of which kills countless ideas and splendid plans; that the moment one definitely commits oneself, then Providence moves too."

What shall we then say to these things? ***If God be for us, who can be against us?***
Romans 8:31(KJV)

We need to lay aside our excuses. The excuse of inadequacy, our lack of ability, that we are naïve, unaware and destitute of knowledge.

If God *be* for us…

One of the reasons I dislike taking my cell phone with me on a run is because someone's inevitably going to call. I hear it ring. I take the call. The sweat is running down my face. The sweat gets on my phone and there's nothing to dry it off with because I'm soaked with perspiration. I didn't look to see if it was one of my contacts, I just answered. It's a wrong number and they hang up.

It hindered my run.

Beloved, when I gave all diligence to write unto you of the common salvation, it was needful for me to write unto you, and exhort you that ye should earnestly ***contend*** *for* ***the faith*** *which was once delivered unto the saints.*
Jude 1:3(KJV)

Sometimes when you're running you have to ***contend*** with all kinds of conditions, circumstances, and environments. We need to get to a place where we reflexively ***go after the goal line, the faith, what we believe.*** We are going to have to labor for, strive for, chase after, run after, and stay in the race until we finish.

In many of the old manuscripts faith is described as "one's strong conviction in the light of his or hers relationship to Christ and their enlightened conscious.

What is my conviction?

Wayne Smith put it into concise and succinct thought in a piece called "My Colors".

MY COLORS ARE CLEAR
Wayne Smith

I am a part of the fellowship of the Unashamed.
- The dye has been cast.
- The decision has been made.

I am a disciple of Jesus Christ.

<u>I won't:</u>
- look back,
- let up,
- slow down,
- back away,
- or be still.
- My past is redeemed,
- and my future is secure.

I am finished and done with:
- low living,
- sight walking,
- small planning,
- colorless dreams,
- tame visions,
- chintzy giving
- and dwarfed goals.

I no longer need:
- preeminence,
- prosperity,
- position,
- promotions,
- plaudits,
- or popularity.

I don't have to be:
- right,
- first,
- tops,
- recognized,
- praised,
- regarded,
- or rewarded.

My pace is set, my goal is Heaven, my road is narrow, my way is rough, my companions few, my Guide is reliable, my mission is clear.

I cannot be:
- bought,
- compromised,
- deterred,
- lured away,
- turned back,
- diluted,
- or delayed.

I will not:
- flinch in the face of sacrifice,
- hesitate in the presence of adversity,
- negotiate at the table of the enemy,
- ponder at the pool of popularity, or
- meander in the maze of mediocrity.

I won't:
- give up,
- back up,
- let up,
- or shut up until:
- I'm prayed up,
- stored up,
- and have stayed up for the cause of Christ.

I am a disciple of Jesus Christ.

I will:
- go until He returns,

- give until I drop
- and work until He comes.

And when He comes to get His own, He will have no problem recognizing me. **My colors will be clear.**

Any questions?

Didn't think so.

That pretty much sums it up, don't you think?

> *Ye did run well; who did hinder…*
> **Galatians 5:7(KJV)**

Got it!!!

OK… no more excuses.

Let's get out there, stretch, and run baby run…

Christians have "simultaneously toned up their bodies and dumbed down their minds."

Os Guinness

Chapter Ten

THE TRUTH ABOUT RUNNING

For he knoweth our frame; he remembereth that we are dust.
Psalms 103:14(KJV)

Some of us are built for running. I just don't happen to be one of them.

Top marathon runners tend to be lean and light. The perfect marathon runner has a light frame, slim legs, and is of small to medium height. They have a high percentage of slow twitch fibers and very high maximal oxygen uptake. They can withstand dehydration, and training gives their muscles a high storage capacity for the premium muscle fuel, glycogen.

The perfect 100 meter sprinter is tall, with a strong mesomorphic body shape. Top sprinters have slim lower legs and relatively narrow hips which gives a biomechanical advantage. They have a high percentage of fast twitch fibers (more than 80%). They use muscle fuel so fast that they are practically running on empty by the end of the race.

Mike Rennie, professor of clinical physiology at the University of Nottingham Medical School in Derby cites the case of identical twins from Germany, one of whom was an endurance athlete, the other a power Sportsman, "They look quite different, despite being identical twins."

My good friend Pastor Irvin McCorkle made the statement: "We are all brothers and sisters just not twins." Thanks Pastor; I needed that.

God knows my frame. He knows what I'm made of. He knows what I inherited through my ancestral genetics, my heredities. He knows what I am and what I've become, and He loves me and cares for me regardless. He understands the distance from Him in which my predecessors, my lineage since Adam including myself has run.

² Thou knowest my downsitting and mine uprising, thou understandest my thought afar off.
³ Thou compassest my path and my lying down, and art acquainted with all my ways.
Psalms 139:2-3(KJV)

He knows when I feel discouraged and depressed. He knows when I lay down in despair. He knows when I get up again and again and go on. He's mindful of the twisted ankle. He knows I'm not just like everybody else.

I know I'm not a special case. We are all different. Not twins. What I struggle with today, you may struggle with tomorrow and every struggle has its own nuance. I've learned that running this race isn't for the lazy, looking for the soft touch and the red carpet treatment without effort. Many of the *Psalms* of *David* were born in difficulty.

Most of the *Epistles* of *Paul* were written in prison. *John Bunyan* wrote *Pilgrim's Progress* from jail. *Florence Nightingale*, too ill to move from her bed, reorganized the hospitals of England.

Semi-paralyzed and under constant menace of apoplexy *(stroke)*, *Louis Pasteur* was tireless in his attack on disease.

During the greater part of his life, American historian *Francis Parkman* suffered so acutely that he could not work for more than five minutes at a time. His eyesight was so wretched that he could scrawl only a few gigantic words on a manuscript, but he contrived to write twenty magnificent volumes of history.

Henri Dunant, a wealthy 19th Century Swiss banker, was sent to Paris by his government to work on a business deal with Napoleon.

But when he arrived he discovered that Napoleon was off fighting a war. So he went to the battlefront to find him. Once there, Durant watched in horror as cannonballs ripped open human flesh. Maimed and dying men lay all around him. He was so devastated by what he saw that he stayed at the front for weeks, helping doctors tend to the wounded.

Even after returning home Durant was haunted by those images of war. He couldn't keep his mind on banking and became so distracted that he lost his fortune. But even with his career in ruins, he had an unmistakable sense of God's leadings in all that had happened.

Later he wrote, "It seemed to me that I had something to accomplish, a sacred duty that was destined to have infinite consequence for mankind." And he was right.

Out of his pain came purpose and Henri Dunant founded the International Committee of the Red Cross (ICRC) in 1863. For establishing it, he received the first Nobel Peace Prize. Clara Barton was a pioneer nurse who founded American the Red Cross and spent her life as a humanitarian.

In a world filled with discrimination you have Booker T. Washington, Marian Anderson, George Washington Carver, and Martin Luther King, Jr.

Christopher Parkening one of the most famous classical guitarists in the world has lived the experience of reaching lofty goals and receiving acclaim for his hard work. But since coming to know Christ midway through his career, Parkening has often remarked, ***True happiness comes when you squander your life for a great purpose.***"

Many others have run this race and won, and we don't even know their names.

We don't want that kind of Jesus Way to rub off on us. It's an uphill road that we run and you're gonna get tired. We don't want to have to go to Samaria and on to Golgotha. As Dorthy Sayers has so astutely said: *"...we have pared the claws of the Lion of Judah. Making Him a fitting household pet for pale curates and pious old ladies."*

I'm sorry, but no pain, no gain. Running isn't easy.

Many runners experience a state of euphoria while running. While the actual state that they feel varies immensely for each individual, there is a common feeling associated with the term "runner's high." When a person is asked about runner's high they typically will say that it's a pleasant state that a runner might experience after a certain distance.

I think I had that "runners high" once back in '65, and no, not 1865.

I have felt the exhilaration of witnessing to someone in need of Christ and then leading that person to Him. I have felt that exhilaration of being in a foreign country ministering the Good News that Christ came to take them as they were and loved them enough not to leave them that way. Now that's a runners high, because you're not running against the wind, your running with the wind at your back.

Then there's the triathlete. A triathlon, in its most popular form, involves swimming, cycling, and running in immediate succession over various distances. Triathletes compete for fastest overall course completion time, including timed "transitions" between the individual swim, cycle, and run components.

I'm tired just thinking about it. These people are incredible.

Just about the time I think I'm busy doing something for the Kingdom, I meet someone who is really busy for the cause of Christ. They must be triathletes for God.

I like the story of the man lying in bed and his wife comes and wakes him up and says to him, *"It's time to get up out of bed."* He says: *"Give me four good reasons why I should get up."* His wife replies, *"OK, one it's morning, second it's Sunday, third we go to church, and fourth you're the Pastor!"*

Everybody gets tired sometimes, even Evangelists. Well I guess I'd better get busy. I haven't even left the house and I'm tired.

Nothing that exists can exist beyond the pale of His presence, nothing is irrelevant to it, nothing is without significance in it...There is never a moment that does not carry eternal significance...no action that is sterile, no love that lacks fruition, and no prayer that is unheard.

Brennan Manning
The Rabbi's Heartbeat

Chapter Eleven

NO EXCUSES

I returned, and saw under the sun, **that the race is not to the swift,** *nor the battle to the strong, neither yet bread to the wise, nor yet riches to men of understanding, nor yet favour to men of skill; but time and chance happeneth to them all.*
Ecclesiastes 9:11(KJV)

When reading this verse keep in mind that the imperative language *time* and *chance* are referring to a *season* and *occurrent event with impact*. The implication being that all of us will have a *moment in time* or a *season in time* that we will either choose for it to *impact* our lives or we will choose to ignore that moment and event. Sometimes what's happening to us may be happening for us.

Winning in life is not about being first; it is about finishing.

My mother was ninety-one when she went home to be with the Lord. She made it a habit to walk everywhere she could. She was into health foods before it was fashionable. She believed that castor oil was good for everything and that aloe vera was good on wounds and bruises. She put wheat germ in her food and rode a three wheeled bike to the store to get her groceries.

I remember one time when my hair started to thin, she said that if I took cayenne pepper and vodka that it would restore my hair loss. I told her that I would try it. Sometime later she ask me if I had tried the formula. I told her that I had. She asked me how I thought it worked and I told her that I put the cayenne pepper on my head and drank the vodka. I thought she was going to have a stroke she was so upset. She told me I was supposed to mix it and put it on my head. I laughed until I couldn't take it anymore and reassured her that I neither took the cayenne pepper nor did I drink the vodka. Needless to say my mom, being a teetotaler, never recommended anything that required alcohol again.

Within the human heart, if we are not careful things begin to take over in our lives that weren't originally intended. The race is on for dominion. In the moral darkness of our lives…stubborn and aggressive usurpers fight among themselves for first place in our hearts for its throne. They will stop us from our objective if we let them.

A. W. Tozer in his book *"The Pursuit Of God"* speaks of an author's words in the old English classic, *"The Cloud Of Unknowing,"* written by an English monk around 1370 AD:

"Lift up thine heart unto God with a meek stirring of love; and mean Himself, and none of His goods. And thereto, look thee… loath to think on aught but God Himself. So that nought work in thy wit, nor in thy will, but

God Himself. This is the work of the soul that most pleaseth God."

The goal of life is Christocentric: to follow Christ, to imitate and resemble Him. To run for Christ is to lose those things that have become our life.

This is a race we all can win. Let's see, what was that commercial? ***"A body in motion stays in motion."***

My momma always said, ***"an idle mind is the devils workshop."***

Time and *chance* simply means everyone will have a moment and an opportunity do something of significance.

Calvin Coolidge (1872-1933), the 30th U.S. President made this poignant statement: *"Press on. Nothing can take the place of persistence. Talent will not. Nothing is more common than unsuccessful men with talent. Genius will not. Unrewarded genius is almost a Proverb. Education will not. The world is full of educated derelicts.* ***Persistence and determination alone are overwhelmingly powerful.****"*

Dean Rhodes was a man who missed opportunity after opportunity. But he didn't make excuses for his shortcomings or whine about what might have been. He kept going.

Here's what I mean: Rhodes met Dave Thomas long before the restaurateur opened his first Wendy's. Rhodes admitted that he always knew the young Thomas would someday do something big. But when given the opportunity to invest in Wendy's, he didn't.

Later, Rhodes met Colonel Sanders and had an opportunity to buy stock in his company before it went national. But he turned that down as well because he didn't agree with some of the colonel's ideas. When Rhodes was in the restaurant equipment business, he often had equipment salesmen in his office trying to sell him on their machines. One of them was Ray Kroc. Rhodes admitted that Kroc was a pleasant person. However, he chose not to invest in the little hamburger stand called McDonald's.

A few years later, on a cruise, he met an attorney from the Pacific Northwest who suggested that Rhodes invest in his new computer company. It had a funny name: Microsoft. Rhodes declined.

Most people would pull their hair out and complain if they missed only of those opportunities, making excuses for why it didn't work out. Not Rhodes.

He saw his mistakes for what they were and focused on pursuing his own dreams and opportunities. Eventually he saw his name at #289 on the Forbes list of the 400 most successful business owners in America (1).

Just because someone is ahead of you doesn't make you a failure. Turn them into an example of what you can or should not do. In school, I wasn't as fast in math as some of my friends, but I always got to the correct bottom line. Don't dwell on how fast or slow you are, just concentrate on the finish line.

Don't avoid the truth. It will set you free. Take ownership of truth. Barbara Johnson states that *"The truth will set you free... but first it will make you miserable"* (2).

I don't necessarily think that truth will always make you miserable, unless you're avoiding it or denying it.

The truth is this: there will always be someone faster, someone with fewer injuries, someone who makes running seem effortless. There will always be someone that we think "I wish I could be like that" or "I wish I could do that" or "I wish I had done or said that." There will always be *that* someone. But who is it that we really need to see and emulate?

For consider him *that endured such contradiction of sinners against himself,* ***lest ye be wearied and faint in your minds.***

Hebrews 12:3(KJV)

You see running is not only physical, but spiritual and mental. Your mind will tell you that you can't finish. That's what the enemy told Jesus, He couldn't finish. His flesh told Him that He couldn't finish, the priest told Him that He couldn't finish, the crowd told Him that He couldn't finish. However, He endured against all the critics. So don't be weary and faint.

Don't panic; panic creates fear and fear can paralyze you. Fear causes the **mind** to start questioning. Fear causes the **will** to lose its leadership and authority. Fear causes the **emotions** to start doubting.

Years ago while in Minnesota during the winter, I held a series of services as a guest speaker and decided one bright sun shiny day to go for a run.

I will insert here for those who know Minnesota winters that though the day was bright, I wasn't. I bundled up, threw a stocking hat on, ear muffs, insulated underwear, a warm coat, shoes and socks, through a scarf around my face and took off. Ladies and gentleman, "Baby, it's cold outside."

In just a few minutes I realized this was a wrong decision. Very wrong. My first indication was the difficulty in the breathing. It seemed as if I couldn't get enough oxygen in my lungs. It didn't take long for the panic and the fear to kick in. My mind, will, and emotions each took their turn and then all together they screamed for help. I remember grabbing at my scarf around my face only to realize that my warm breath clashing with the cold air had created a freeze zone on the scarf close to my mouth and all I had to do was just move it around. My fear had me imagining myself dead from the freezing temperature and not found until spring. Remember when it comes to our fears:

Many of our fears are:
- Fears about the future which never happen
- Fears about the past that cannot be changed
- Fears about our health that will never occur

- Fears that can be overcome and conquered by appropriate action

    Let's see… what was that saying? "Don't panic on the minds side because of pressure from the outside, because we have a presence on the inside and a power alongside." God is the equivalent to the requirement.

    At a meeting several years ago, Dr. George Woods shared this story. While on a tour trip with his wife and friends, he decided to read while they were traveling by bus to another location. After sometime reading, Dr. Woods removed his glasses to rest his eyes. Upon returning his glasses to his eyes he noticed his right eye was blurry. Dr. Wood was immediately alarmed. After refocusing several times, he determined that he had been afflicted with a minor stroke. In an effort not to alarm his wife and friends, whom he knew would want him to seek immediate medical attention, stayed to himself during lunch, insisting his wife and friends continue to fellowship through lunch.

    While contemplating his situation, he proceeded to be angry with himself, that he had allowed this to happen and angry at God for allowing this to take place.

    At that moment the tour guide came up and addressed Dr. Woods, *"Dr. Woods,"* the tour guide said, **"I found the lens to the right side of your glasses."**

    In the humanity of **Jesus** we behold **the mystery of eternity and why we contend for the faith.**

Ernst Renan could not believe that and wrote wistfully of Jesus in the past tense: *"But he is dead and for hence he lies, in that forlorn Assyrian town, and on his grave with shining eyes, the Syrian stars look down."*

However, **later, Renan began to explore the ultimate powers of life** that can make sense of this senseless life "full of sound and fury," a tale told by an idiot and he came up against one answer. **Jesus, the man for all, who suffered for all, who conquered the prison of death is the only foundation of truth** on which we are able to stand. **Renan said of Jesus: "No one can get behind him, above him, around him. Jesus has become a philosophical absolute."**

I remember my mother singing an old gospel hymn, "To Be Like Jesus."

> To be like Jesus, to be like Jesus
> All I ask is to be like Him;
> All through life's journey
> From earth to glory
> All I ask is to be like Him;
> Not in a measure but in its fullness
> All I ask is to be like Him.

I know that in trying to emulate Christ, I will fail in any perfected appearance. But thankfully Christ bridges the gaps of my life and becomes the bridge across the great abyss of my sins, mistakes, and failures.

Gonna keep on running I can't stop now.

These words of wisdom were found on the wall of Mother Teresa's room in Calcutta, India,

"People are often unreasonable, irrational, and self-centered. Forgive them anyway. If you are kind, people may accuse you of selfish, ulterior motives. Be kind anyway. If you are successful, you will win some unfaithful friends and some genuine enemies. Succeed anyway. If you are honest and sincere people may deceive you. Be honest and sincere anyway. What you spend years creating, others could destroy overnight. Create anyway. If you find serenity and happiness, some may be jealous. Be happy anyway. The good you do today, will often be forgotten. Do good anyway. Give the best you have, and it will never be enough. Give your best anyway. In the final analysis, it is between you and God. It was never between you and them anyway."

Chapter Twelve

RUNNING WITH GRACE

A man was once quoted as saying, *"The more I know people the better I like my dog."* I've thought that a few times. And I don't even have a dog.

A minister once said, *"I could really enjoy the ministry if it wasn't for people."*

You're going to **run into people,** so you had better run with grace.

*For by **grace**: ……. it is the gift of God*
Ephesians 2:8 (KJV)

*…God is able to make **all grace abound** toward you*
1 Corinthians 9:8 (KJV)

*And he said unto me, **My grace is sufficient** …*
2 Corinthians 12:9 (KJV)

I often tell people that the ***Grace will keep you where the Faith of God will lead you***. Grace is **G**ods **R**edemption **A**t **C**hrist's **E**xpense. It is interesting to me that in looking at the word Grace that the bulk of the word (Grace) is **RACE**. From the center to the circumference God is trying to create one people, with one mind and one purpose and that is to **Run this Race by His Grace**.

The Apostle Paul relays to us and for us that he understands that we are in what the French would say *C'est la guerre* – *'that's war.'*

*[5] For, when we were come into Macedonia, our flesh had no rest, but we were **troubled** on every side; **without were fightings, within were fears.***
*[6] **Nevertheless God, that comforteth** those that are cast down, **comforted us by the coming of Titus***
2 Corinthians 7:5-6 (KJV)

Running has its challenges. There will always be obstacles on the course. You will from time to time call it an obstacle course, because it is an engagement that will endeavor to turn you back. There will be troubling encounters, **without were fightings** and *fears within*. However, God will always provide a Titus for us or as the Greeks would have it, a **paraclete or** *para-kle-tos*, one who comes alongside, who understands the situation, the circumstances, and the condition.

*But the **Comforter**, (para-kle-tos) which is the Holy Ghost, whom the Father will send in my name, he shall **teach you all things**, and **bring all things to your remembrance**, whatsoever I have said unto you.*
John 14:26(KJV)

Our *parakletos,* the Holy Spirit of God, will not only **teach** us but will remind us, bring us into **remembrance** that we cannot only finish, but we can win.

It was always encouraging for me to have another runner come along side and encourage me. And sometimes I would come alongside a runner and run with them for a distance and give someone comradery, that feeling of closeness like soldiers who have experienced the sound and the fury of war zones.

... Not by might, nor by power, but by my spirit, saith the LORD of hosts.
Zechariah 4:6 (KJV)

"A distinguished foreigner was a big help to the American colonists during the Revolutionary War," the history teacher said. "Can you give me his name, Tommy?"
"God," Tommy answered.

E. Stanley Jones (1884–1973) was a 20th-century Methodist Christian missionary and theologian who stated without equivocation, *"Anything less than God will let you down."* Remember rough weather won't last, but tough people will.
God's Grace is stronger than sin because God's Grace is Christ. God's crowning achievement is our greatest victory.

Monroe Bartlett Senior (1885-1941) wrote a song that reminds us of our Victory through Christ.

Victory in Jesus
I heard an old, old story,
How a Savior came from glory,
How He gave His life on Calvary
To save a wretch like me;
I heard about His groaning,
Of His precious blood's atoning,
Then I repented of my sins
And won the victory.

Refrain:
O victory in Jesus,
My Savior, forever.
He sought me and bought me
With His redeeming blood;
He loved me ere I knew Him,
And all my love is due Him,
He plunged me to victory,
Beneath the cleansing flood.

I've said it many times and I will keep on saying it because it's true. The poet Emerson laid it out: "What lies before us and what lies behind us is only minor compared to what lies within us."

Running with Grace is understanding that it's not by our might or by our power, but it is by God's spirit. He will be the wind, the breath that will compel you to go on. This race is a lifelong journey and there is an inner voice that will try to get you to stop and give up. I know that voice tried to get me to lie down, stop, quit, or die. I would have had it not been for His Grace. I would have laid down and slept the great sleep but for the voice of Grace: "*And he said unto me, My **grace** is sufficient for thee*" (**2 Corinthians 12:9**).

My wife Paula some time ago while going through a period of anguish wrote a piece that speaks volumes to all of us. "*... I speak now with my inner voice... not my everyday voice that you would recognize, but my other voice, the one from the deep recesses of my soul. This voice resonates loudly from the very deepest part of me, where the wound is most tender. The cry is from my storm shelter, where I go when it hurts. This voice, when spoken, makes my being tremble like an earthquake that has shook the entirety of my world. This voice wants to be heard. It will no longer remain silent. This other voice, this inner voice shouts 'I need His grace'*"

My **race**, my journey into His Grace and restoration has been a long and rough path of my own making. Health for the soul doesn't always come easy.

The prayers of my church, family, and friends have helped me keep my spiritual equilibrium and connection with God on every level of my march to victory. Now my running, my race is not *to* victory but *in* victory.

If God cannot be the God of my future, then He cannot be God at all. Now my future cannot be halted by the mistakes of my past, only hindered. We all have a private and personal hell that no one wants to hear or talk about. Our anger, frustration, and the manipulation of others that we have all felt in our lives has now, because of

God's Grace, made us stronger in our journey. I can feel His strength in my spirit cruising through my soul. I am not alone on this run.

My lifelong friend and Pastor O. C. Philips observed, "There are no orphans in God and no grandchildren. Only children." I find great comfort in these words.

I am thankful to God, that there are no orphans in Him. This thought, brings me peace and hope. It reminds me that I belong and I'm not alone.

Take a long look around you at a fast paced world that's running with its eyes closed. They have eyes and can't see the collision that lies ahead. Look around you and you will see the many orphans belonging to man's inhumanity to man, lying strewn and scattered across the human landscape.

I was in Mumbai, India many years ago in a crusade. I can see them now. The streets were lined with people who had been orphaned by life. My journeys throughout the world opened my eyes.

Several years ago an article in the LA Times had this headline: "He Died in Vast Isolation." Vincenzo Ricardo. If that name does not mean much to you, you are not alone. It does not seem to have meant much to anyone else except, perhaps, him who bore it. In fact, it was not even his name. His real name was Vincenzo Riccardi, and nobody seemed to get it right after the sensational discovery of his mummified body in Southampton, New York. He had been dead for 13 months, but his television was still on, and his body was propped up in a chair in front of it. The television was his only companion, and though it had much to tell him, it did not care whether he lived or died.

Riccardi's story raises many unsettling questions. How can a human being vanish for over a year and not be missed by anyone?

Where was his family? What about his relatives?

Why was the power still on in his house? Whatever the answers are to these and other questions, one thing is clear: Riccardi was a lonely individual whose life can be summed up in one word, alienation. You see, Riccardi was blind, so he never really watched television; he needed this virtual reality to feed his need for real companionship (1).

There are many who "Suffer in Silence." If you listen closely, you can hear their inner voices. They are running for their lives. They just don't know where to run. I wonder on whose shoulders that weight belongs. No one has cared enough to ask them about their own journey…and, even if someone did ask, they're afraid to speak for themselves. Their lips are sealed with fear because someone might discover their pain. These are the ones who "Suffer in Silence." We can't let that happen. We must become more aware and discerning because there are hurting orphans everywhere and age isn't a factor here.

There are pasts to keep hidden and stories untold that cause loss, separation, divorce, families estranged from one another, children asking 'why' and parents, families, friends, leaders, politicians *running* out of answers.

I see the aftermath of a bloody battle ground, the dead and the wounded are lying everywhere. They are there because no one came in time to stop the bleeding and the dying. Over there is one of the wounded who suffered at the feet of someone who was unforgiving of mistakes and failures. And over there is another wounded soul devastated by life and there, and over there, and the list of the walking wounded just keeps growing.

Who's going to help them to the finish line?

The Pharisee mentality might stop to say, "Hey, I love you… I forgive you, but I'm sorry. I can't stop now. It's far too risky. It might take time and effort, and I'm too busy. I might feel compelled to help, give a word of encouragement or put a healing salve on the wound… Oh my! Look at the time…***gotta run***." And then there's always the one who stoops down, to whisper in the ear of the wounded and say, "you know, you're just getting what you deserve."

I ask you, who is there to help? Me? Us? Can we? Can we hear them? Can we feel their pain? Can we speak to the barely alive, and gently ask them what hurts and where? Can we help them ***run again***? This is an intentional path for the brave and courageous. Orphans themselves cannot go alone. Who is it that can continue without help? Who can continue this unsightly walk of the living dead and the walking wounded?

Who can stop long enough to grieve over the bones bleaching in the desert of the un-named and unrecognized? Placing them in coffins of gold doesn't give the journey value. Only the ones who have been there and have stopped to help can give their journey value and answers, they know, *they've run this path before*.

Lord, help me offer the fallen my intentional human and God given compassion. I pray for those who have fallen from Grace and those who have not fallen from Grace …that we would together **fall on thy Grace**.

Thy Grace is sufficient.

Late have I loved Thee, O Beauty so ancient and so new, late have I loved Thee! And behold, Thou wert within and I was without. I was looking for Thee out there, and I threw myself, deformed as I was, upon those well-formed things which Thou hast made. These things held me from Thee...Thou didst call and cry out and burst in upon my deafness; Thou didst shine forth and glow and drive away my blindness; Thou didst send forth Thy fragrance and I drew in my breath, and now I pant for Thee; I have tasted and now I hunger and thirst; Thou didst touch me, and I was inflamed with desire for Thy peace. When I shall cleave to Thee with all my being...my life will be alive, wholly filled with Thee.

AUGUSTINE, CONFESSIONS
(Book X section 38)

Chapter Thirteen

RUN DOWN

There's a feeling sometimes that occurs when you're doing things you enjoy. You're moving along the way you did yesterday but today it seems more difficult. Your energy seems gone. You feel *run down*.
Let's see... I took my supplements, drank plenty of water, and ate a banana, but man I feel *run down*.
I did my devotions, I prayed, but somehow it just didn't seem enough. Something is just off kilter.

"Thou wert within and I was without. I was looking for Thee out there, and I threw myself, deformed as I was, upon those well-formed things which Thou hast made."

Augustine

There is a story about a man on his knees, crawling with his hands in front of him, carefully probing the lighted circle. After a few moments a policeman walks by, seeing the man on all fours. The policeman poses the obvious question: **"Did you lose something?"**
"Yes," the man replies. **"I have lost my keys."**
Kindly, the police officer joins in the man's search, and the two now circle the lighted area on hands and knees.
But after some time, the officer stops. **"Are you absolutely certain this is where you lost your keys? We've covered every inch."**

"**Why no,**" the man replies matter-of-factly, pointing to a darkened corner. "**I lost them over there.**" The policeman is visibly shaken. "**Well then why in the name of all heaven are we looking for them over here?**" The man responds with equal annoyance: "**Isn't that obvious? The light is better over here!**"

It is far easier to limit our search for life's missing keys to easy, comfortable places. Searching dark and difficult corners—where the keys may have, in fact, been lost—is far less desirable (1).

We must be aware that our weariness, that *run down* feeling may be coming from something biding for our attention, trying to distract us from what we are doing and where we are going.

A. W. Tozer made this penetrating observation: "The more a man has in his own heart the less he will require from the outside; excessive need for support from without is proof of the bankruptcy of the inner man."

Our bankruptcy empties us and drains us of our drive, our hunger to run. We tend to feel a sense of spiritual inertia. Apathy starts to creep in. We want to care, we want to keep our hopes and aspirations high, however they seem to dissipate and dissolve into nothingness.

Charles Swindoll relates how every time he hears the word apathy, he remembers a friend who taught high school just long enough to realize he shouldn't have been teaching high school. It took him several years to come to that realization.

He was assigned to teach a course filled to the brim with students who did not want to learn. In fact, it was one of those classes where you had to arrive very early to get a back seat. A couple of the fellas got there so late, they were stuck on the front row. There they sat in their cutoffs and sneakers without socks. They couldn't care less what the subject was.

The teacher finally got fed up with their apathy. He grabbed a piece of chalk, whirled around to the chalkboard and began to slash away in big, foot-high letters, "A-P-A-T-H-Y!" He underlined it twice, then slammed an exclamation point on it that broke the chalk as he hammered it against the board.

One of the dull students up front frowned as he struggled to read the word. Unable to pronounce it, he tilted his head to one side as he started spelling it aloud, "A-P-A-T-H-Y." He mispronounced it, "ay-pay-thee." Then he leaned over and muttered to his buddy, "What in the world is 'ay-pay-thee'?" His friend yawned back with a sigh, "Who cares?" (2)

When we feel *run down* we begin to think, *nobody seems to care. So why should I?*

Life ceases to be tragic. Life becomes simply dull.

H. L. Mencken said it well, "The basic fact about human experience is not that it is a tragedy, but that it is a bore. It is not that it is predominantly painful, but that it is lacking in any sense."

No one ever said it better than Thoreau: "Most men lead lives of quiet desperation."

Apathy must be replaced with action.
Pacifism with passion.
Lethargy with alertness.
Inactivity with pro-activity.

This we must guard against in our Christian experience, **in our running for Christ.** Brennan Manning makes this poignant statement: "The pressures of religious conformity and political correctness in our culture bring us face to face with what Johannes Metz called **'the poverty of uniqueness.' The poverty of uniqueness is the call of Jesus to stand utterly alone when the only alternative is to cut a deal at the price of one's integrity.**"

We must fight against being spiritually and morally bankrupt. Sometime ago Gordon MacDonald authored a book entitled "Restoring Your Spiritual Passion." MacDonald named three things essential to recovering passion when experiencing lost purpose, clouded vision, or confused direction: an address book with the names of "special friends who encourage you to obey God," a map indicating the location of "safe places where you rediscover who God is," and a calendar marking "still times when you hear what God says."

We should be comrades in arms on the war of spiritual poverty and moral bankruptcy.

We have allowed the world to redefine faith to something less than what it was meant to be.

There is a phrase in Latin that summarizes the idea that the way our minds and souls are oriented is the way our lives are oriented. *Lex orandi, lex credendi, lex vivendi* is an axiom of ancient Christianity, meaning: the rule of worship is the rule of belief is the rule of life.

Howard Macey makes the profound statement: "The spiritual life cannot be made suburban. It is always frontier and we who live in it must accept and even rejoice that it remains untamed."

It is imperative that we realize our faith in Christ is essential to combating that *run down* feeling, realizing that this comes from what Augustine of Hippo defines as a soul "too cramped" for God to enter. He prayed that God might widen and empty it. "You prompt us yourself to find satisfaction in appraising you," he prayed. "[Y]ou made us tilted toward you, and our heart is unstable until stabilized in you" (3).

Floyd McClung in his book *"Finding Friendship With God"* makes this observation:

"You wake up one morning and all your spiritual feelings are gone. You pray, but nothing happens. You rebuke the devil, but it doesn't change anything.

You go through spiritual exercises, you have your friends pray for you, you confess every sin you can imagine, then go around asking forgiveness of everyone you know... You begin to wonder how long this spiritual gloom might last. Days? Weeks? Months? Will it ever end? ...it feels that your prayers simply bounce off the ceiling. In utter desperation you cry out, 'What's the matter with me?'"

*Put on the whole armour of God, that ye may be able to stand against the **wiles** of the devil.*
                                    Ephesians 6:11 (KJV)

- ***Wiles*** - methodeia, meth-od-i'-ah; (trickery):--wile, technique, or process. Cunning arts, deceit, craft.

There are reasons that we feel *run down,* physically, psychologically, and spiritually.

In Schultz's comic Peanuts, in his book "Searching For The Meaning Of Life," Linus is talking to Snoopy. *"Here's something to think about,"* Linus says. *"Life is like a ten-speed bicycle, Most of us have gears that we never use!"*

To which Snoopy responds, *"He's wrong...that isn't something to think about..."*

We must however understand some of the things that not only lie before us but what lies within us.

Sometimes we mistake a *physical problem as a spiritual problem*. Being physically *run down* can be misinterpreted as being somehow spiritually inept.

An example: A Christian may be taken ill by some condition or disease and may not be aware of it. All they know is that they do not feel as they used to feel.

A kind of fatigue overtakes them. They do not feel or enjoy reading the Bible as they used to; they cannot pray as they used to; they are depressed. They cannot understand this, and the ADVERSARY comes to them and suggests that it is because they are slipping in a spiritual sense. The ENEMY may even raise the question as to whether they have ever been spiritual at all. The ENEMY suggests that this is purely a spiritual problem and that God is somehow displeased with them, and that they are being punished. They become tormented, discouraged, defeated. We forget that bad things happen to good people.

In our age of husbands and wives working long hours and the many demands of making ends meet, the zest of life can be beaten out of you. Understand when you are physically down, it is hard to be spiritually up.

Then there is mistaking *psychological problems* for *spiritual problems*. People are born with different temperaments and that doesn't change when they get born again. For instance, some people get up in the morning flying high, others get up a little at a time.

I am reminded of a prayer I once read:

Dear Lord,

So far today, God, I've done all right. I haven't gossiped, haven't lost my temper, haven't been greedy, grumpy, nasty, selfish, or over-indulgent. I'm really glad about that.
But in a few minutes, God, I'm going to get out of bed, and from then on I'm probably going to need a lot more help.
Amen.

Some people have more outgoing personalities than others. Just know there is a difference. Don't beat yourself up because you're not like another Christian. Don't let the ENEMY condemn you or put you on a GUILT trip because you are not like some else.

Some can get so spiritually excited that they could run and swing from a chandelier, but that does not make them any more spiritual than the person who doesn't do that. Bishop G. E. Patterson said, "Some people are just releasing energy."

Now there are some Christians who have *Spiritual* problems, but try to make them *physical* or *psychological* problems. Many Christians have a tendency to evade spiritual problems. When you don't want to face the truth, you have a spiritual problem. When you don't want disciplines in your life, then you have a spiritual problem. When you don't want to obey the principles of God's Word, you have a spiritual problem. The ENEMY will do whatever he can to keep you from facing the truth.

Allow me to give you three brief responses to help you when facing these problematic areas.

If you have *physical problems* and your *feeling run down*, get the saints to pray for you or find a doctor.

Is any sick among you? let him call for the elders of the church; and let them pray over him, anointing him with oil in the name of the Lord.
James 5:14 (KJV)

If you have *psychological problems* and feeling *run down*, seek answers.

⁹*And I say unto you, Ask, and it shall be given you; seek, and ye shall find; knock, and it shall be opened unto you.* ¹⁰*For every one that asketh receiveth; and he that seeketh findeth; and to him that knocketh it shall be opened.*
Luke 11:9-10 (KJV)

If you have *spiritual problems* and you're feeling *run down*, find Christ. Then admit it, quit it, and forget it.

⁸*But what saith it? The word is nigh thee, even in thy mouth, and in thy heart: that is, the word of faith, which we preach;* ⁹*That if thou shalt confess with thy mouth the Lord Jesus, and shalt believe in thine heart that God hath raised him from the dead, thou shalt be saved.* ¹⁰*For with the heart man believeth unto righteousness; and with the mouth confession is made unto salvation.* ¹¹*For the scripture saith, Whosoever believeth on him shall not be ashamed.*
Romans 10:8-11 (KJV)

There will always be those who are so spiritually minded, they're no earthly good.

The opposite of Christlikeness is not sinfulness like we might expect, but apathy. The idea that follows is that even the worst sinner who cries out to God is actually closer to the heart of Christ than the one who stands apathetically. The woman caught in adultery and clinging to the feet of Christ was far closer to the breath of God than the religious men with rocks beside her.

I'm beginning to feel better. I don't feel so *run down.* I think I can finish now.

Yes, I see it now. The finish line is just a head. Just a few more steps and I'm there. Ah! Yes, the scarlet ribbon. I can break through to the other side. I can finish the course. There have been obstacles but my Heavenly Father helped carry me over the finish line.

Ahhhh! Now to rest.

Longing to be important opposes our learning to be significant.

EPILOGUE

RUNNING IN PLACE

I've tried those running and walking machines in the gym. They are without doubt wonderful pieces of equipment to help and aid people; I have just never enjoyed them. I feel confined. It's not a criticism, just a preference. If I lived somewhere like Alaska or Death Valley, California, or any place that cold or hot I would probably want one.

It's the *running in place* that I dislike. You're just not going anywhere and the scenery will always be the wall. Even if you have some kind of interactive monitor in front of you, you're still just there and the interactive monitor isn't like being outside.

When Dick Hoyt's son Richard was born, the umbilical cord was wrapped around his neck. He was brain-damaged; he would never be able to walk or speak.

Dick and his wife brought Richard home to care for him.

When he was eleven, they took him to the engineering department at Tufts University to see if a device could be invented to help him communicate. They were told that his brain was incapable of comprehension.

"Tell him a joke," Dick said. When they did, Richard laughed.

The department constructed a computer that allowed Richard to laboriously type out a sentence by hitting a button with the side of his head—the only part of his body he could move.

When Richard heard one day about a benefit race being run to help a young man who had been paralyzed, he typed out a sentence: ***Dad, I want to run.***

By this time Dick was forty, a self-described porker who had never run over a mile.

He somehow pushed his son in a wheelchair over the course.

Afterward, Richard wrote the sentence that changed Dick's life: ***When I ran, I didn't feel disabled.***

Dick began to run. This strong father has push his son ***over two hundred triathlons.***

More than eighty-five times Dick has pushed Richard's wheelchair the 26.2 miles that make up a marathon.

Dick's best time is a little over two and a half hours— ***within thirty minutes of the world's record,*** which was not set by a guy pushing his son in a wheelchair.

Dick Hoyt said that ***his hero, his inspiration, his courage, his reason for running is the 110-pound motionless, speechless body of the man in the chair, his son*** (1).

You can't do that ***running in place.*** Calvary can't be reached by ***running in place.***

Henry Ford once said that ***"If you do what you always done you'll get what you always got."***

Jesus was born in Bethlehem. He first left the splendor of Heaven. He had to go to Calvary. He made a way. He gave you a map. He cut the road out for you. He stands at the door and knocks. You have to *get up and answer the door*. You have to go to the Cross. It's required. It's where we die to self. It's where we take up the cross and follow Him. It's where we learn to serve others.

Arthur Eddington is one of the founders of the modern science of astronomy. **Eddington's** problem was fitting Christian doctrines, and religion as a whole, into his skeptical scientific view of the created world. Particularly, he thought the incarnation of God in the man Jesus was naïve nonsense.

One day, walking on a beach, he saw a marvelous colony of ants at work. He knew that the seasonal high tides were going to inundate the colony.

"How," he thought to himself, **"could I forewarn the ants of their impending disaster of flooding?"**

The more he thought about it, the more he came to realize, he would have to communicate the knowledge of his truth in ways and means the ants could comprehend. Ants don't have radios. Ants don't know English. So, could he use natural means, such as buckets of water appropriately sloshed around the anthill?

Finally, he concluded, *"Science knows that ants communicate with ants. If I could become an ant and use their form of communiqués, and tell them the truth, then they would listen and act in new ways. They would be saved from destruction."*

Suddenly, Eddington was caught in his own net. Eddington's **main complaint about Christianity was that it was a religion that thought an Almighty Creator**

would speak as a Man to mankind. He came to realize, that's the only way it could be done. He also thought, *"If I spoke to the ants, what if they did not believe me? Would the ants' rejection of my word mean that it was wrong or not truth? Of course not."* This was the clincher for Eddington, **WHY WOULD GOD** want to disclose his concerns to humanity, or in the illustration, why would he, Eddington, want to communicate the truth and reality of life to the anthill?

He could think of only one motive: *"LOVE"* (2).

We are in a constant state of flux. The Greek philosopher Heraclitus said, *"You never step into the same river twice, because the river is in constant change."* Then the Greek philosopher Cratylus said, *"Not only do you not step into the same river twice, you do not even step into the same river once."* Why? *"Because the river is not the only thing that's changing; you are changing as well."*

You can change your mind. You can change your attitude. You can change your friends. You can change many things… but only God can change your eternity.

I'm running on for Jesus. Who are you running for?

When you need help, He's always there.

Excuse me, now I'm headed out the door. Christ has been waiting for me. Together we're going to run the distance.

SOURCE PAGE

CHAPTER THREE
(1) Ravi Zacharias, "Can Man Live Without God"; autobiographical excerpt quoted by Ian Hunter in "Malcolm Mugger-idge: A Life" (Toronto: Totem, 1981, 40)
(2) Stephen Crane, "The Red Badge of Courage" (1894)

CHAPTER FIVE
(1) The West Australian, "Straggling bull gores Pamplona survival guide author" (July 9, 2014). Matt Woodley, editor, preachingtoday.com
(2) Lisa Gutierrez, "Idiot' takes selfie during Spain's Running of the Bulls", The Kansas City Star (July 14, 2014)
(3) Ravi Zacharias, "Cries Of The Heart"
(4) John Maxwell, "Developing The Leader Within"

CHAPTER SIX
(1) John Maxwell, "Failing Forward" (162)

CHAPTER SEVEN
(1) Neil Simon, "The Play Goes On"
(2) CS Lewis, "A Grief Observed"
(3) Leith Anderson, "Winning the Values War in a Chang-ing Culture"; Eileen Cronin-Noe, "Thalidomide Baby Counts Blessings," (Minneapolis Star Tribune, August 2, 1987)

CHAPTER NINE
(1) Dr. Michael Anderson, "This Day"

CHAPTER ELEVEN
(1) John Maxwell "Failing Forward" (172)
(2) Barbara Johnson, "So Let God"

CHAPTER TWELVE
(1) Erika Hayasaki, "He Died in Vast Isolation" (LA Times, March 31, 2007)

CHAPTER THIRTEEN
(1) Jill Carattini, "Where the Light is Strong" (September 17, 2007)
(2) Charles Swindol, "Living On The Ragged Edge"
(3) Saint Augustine, "Confessions", trans. Garry Wills, (New York: Penguin, 2006)

EPILOGUE
(1) John Ortberg "Who Is This Man"
(2) Dr. Michael Anderson, "This Is The Day"